VIRGINIA WOOLF'S LONDON

VIRGINIA WOOLF'S
LONDON

by Dorothy Brewster

GREENWOOD PRESS, PUBLISHERS
WESTPORT, CONNECTICUT

Library of Congress Cataloging in Publication Data

Brewster, Dorothy, 1883-
   Virginia Woolf's London.

   Reprint of the 1960 ed. published by New York Uni-
versity Press, New York.
   Bibliography: p.
   Includes index.
   1. Woolf, Virginia Stephen, 1882-1941--Knowledge--
England. 2. London--Description--1901-1950. I. Title.
[PR6045.072Z563 1979]   823'.9'12   78-26590
ISBN 0-313-20788-7

823.91
W913xbr2

Published in 1960 by New York University Press

Reprinted with the permission of George Allen &
Unwin Ltd., London

Reprinted in 1979 by Greenwood Press, Inc.
51 Riverside Avenue, Westport, CT 06880

Printed in the United States of America

10 9 8 7 6 5 4 3 2 1

INTRODUCTION

'Life,' wrote Virginia Woolf, in an often quoted passage from her essay 'Modern Fiction' in *The Common Reader*, 'is not a series of gig-lamps symmetrically arranged; life is a luminous halo, a semi-transparent envelope surrounding us from the beginning of consciousness to the end. Is it not the task of the novelist to convey this varying, this unknown and uncircumscribed spirit . . . with as little mixture of the alien and external as possible?'

It is difficult to fit London, massive and material and external, into the conception of life as a 'luminous halo'. If admitted at all, Mrs Woolf's London must be very different, one would think, from the London of Dr Johnson or Thackeray or Dickens; more like an insubstantial pageant than a city that can be mapped in a guide-book. Yet her London is abundantly, though not always precisely, identifiable. As she continued her experiments in breaking the mould of conventional fiction, she found the 'external' much more difficult to dispose of than she had thought in 1924, when in *Mr Bennett and Mrs Brown* she condemned the excessively factual structure of the novels of her older contemporaries, Bennett, Wells and Galsworthy, and tried to strip her Mrs Brown in the railway carriage of all external wrappings, and so reveal 'the spirit of life itself'. By 1928, as she notes in her *Diary* (November 28th), she is asking the question, 'What is my own position towards the inner and the outer? What I want now to do is to saturate every atom . . . to give the moment whole; whatever it includes.' To be included—and this the *Diary* makes clear—were the fruits of her endlessly fascinated observation of London ; and to be explored was the relationship between the myriad impressions of London crowds and

7

streets and parks, and the mind and imagination of the observer—herself, and by transference, the characters in her novels. London is a very large part of that 'external' to be absorbed in 'the moment', and so cease to be alien to the uncircumscribed spirit of life.

During her years of London living, Mrs Woolf noted down in her *Diary* details of places and people that interested her in her walks: brief vivid descriptions, reflections and emotions and associations stirred by what she saw. Sometimes the connection between such entries and her later use of them in her critical and creative writing is easily traced. For instance, she walked across Hungerford Bridge one day in April, 1919, and saw the city through the eyes of Defoe, about whom she was writing a review, published later in the month in the *Times Literary Supplement*. The *Diary* describes the view; the conclusion of the essay makes the comparison with Defoe: 'The view of London from Hungerford Bridge, grey, serious, massive, prosaic if it were not for the masts of the ships and the towers and domes of the city, brings him to mind. The tattered girls with violets in their hands at the street corners, and the old weatherbeaten women patiently displaying their matches and bootlaces beneath the shelter of arches, seem like characters from his books.' By the time she wrote *Orlando*, she was expert in the use of London imagery to suggest literary history—imagery evoking the spirit of an age or the essence of a writer. She does not then do anything so prosaic as to describe a London scene and say it 'brings to mind' Dr Johnson and Bolt Court.

As Mrs Woolf develops new ways of expressing the relationship between the 'inner' and 'outer', the part London plays in the lives of her characters is more subtly conceived. In an early novel like *Night and Day*, London is often little more than a setting, the background, described by the author herself, or perceived by the actors as the place where they happen

Introduction

to be. In later books it is so woven into the texture of their experience that it is no easy matter to trace the pattern, and say definitely that Virginia Woolf's London is this and that, like a completed picture puzzle with all its bits in place. The roar of traffic in the Strand or Kingsway falls differently on different ears in different circumstances. The British Museum, St Paul's, Trafalgar Square—their domes and lions and statues—keep their physical identity, but change their atmosphere and significance as they enter the consciousness of Jacob or Bernard or Virginia Woolf herself. There is no finished canvas to place in a literary museum, signed Virginia Woolf. There are impressions, shifting patterns, factual details and flights of metaphor, experiments in shaping the globe of the perfect moment. A suggestion in one book is developed in another, an experiment is dropped and picked up again and carried through elsewhere. Certain London landmarks persist, even through the centuries. There is recurrence with change. We come to distinguish Virginia Woolf's London from the London of other writers, and see the Strand churches through her eyes as she saw the view from Hungerford Bridge through the eyes of Defoe. It is the London of Mrs Dalloway, of Jacob, of Flush, of Orlando, of Eleanor Pargiter, and yet of them all.

Perhaps quite a few devoted readers of Virginia Woolf would agree on a very general characterization of this London. Let one reader risk it, before examining the books in detail and seeing how one aspect of her art develops through a quarter of a century. Her London—like Wordsworth's seen from Westminster Bridge—is a city of 'ships, towers, domes, theatres and temples', open to the sky, not shrouded in fog. The visibility is usually good; it is no *Bleak House* London of rain and mud and mist, murky shadows and hidden pest-holes. There are red and fitful sunsets, staining windows in Park Lane gold, making the long windows in Kensington Palace

9

Introduction

flush fiery rose, bathing streets in a tawny troubled light, thick with the dust of many wheels, turning the Thames into muddy gold. Afternoons in summer are drenched in light sifting down through the trees in the parks. At dusk there are lamps in the windows in the squares, and later the streets are starred with lamps, and there is a race of lights as the buses swerve around curves. There are special effects of light from the flaming bonfire on Guy Fawkes night on Parliament Hill, and from the bonfires of cedar and oak wood, lavishly salted, burning with green, orange and purple fire on the frozen Thames during the Great Frost. (But we are straying into the London of Orlando, not an everyday place). Seen from a ship moving down the river, London is a swarm of lights, with a pale yellow canopy drooping above it.

In the Park on some of those sunny afternoons, the roar of London encircles the open space in a ring of distant sound. In the midst of the traffic of the noonday streets, the separate sounds are 'churned into one sound, steel blue, circular'. (This is the language of *The Waves*). From the river comes the hollow misty cry of steamers. The strokes of Big Ben punctuate the hours of day and night; and the great clock of St Paul's scatters the pigeons and the sparrows. Pigeons coo throughout *The Years;* cries of old iron and rags from the back streets penetrate into the Chelsea drawing-room; and at almost any time and place one may hear a barrel organ or a brass band or a street musician. The unemployed sing in a demonstration and voices proclaim justice and liberty from Hyde Park platforms.

Life flows through the streets, flows into the Underground, flows over the bridges. The crowds streaming incessantly back and forth over Waterloo and Westminster and London Bridge are not those of Mr Eliot's Unreal City—death has not undone them in six hundred years. The flow of time as well as the flow of human life is inseparable from the im-

Introduction

pression of Virginia Woolf's London. At any moment one may be reminded of the long past of the city by some association or some image. It is not only in *Orlando* that the past is made present to the imagination. And before there was a city there was a river and a shore. In an imagined flight over London, the passenger sees right down through the Bank of England; all the business houses are transparent, the river is as the Romans saw it, as paleolithic man saw it at dawn from a hill shaggy with wood, with the rhinoceros digging its horn into the roots of rhododendrons. Indications of the past are not put up like sign-boards. Mrs Woolf will not tell you as you walk through the streets with some of her characters that Hazlitt died in this house in Frith Street, or that Lady Hamilton lived here in Clarges Street. Plaques placed on the wall by the London County Council or some other benevolent authority will do that for you. You will not see them unless you develop the habit Henry James called perambulation.

To suggest how some such general impression of London grows in our minds as we read the novels and essays in their chronological order is the main purpose of the following chapters. They offer a London adventure. They also perhaps throw some light from a special angle on the artistic problem that so challenged Virginia Woolf's imagination—'the combination of the external and the internal'.

ACKNOWLEDGMENTS

The author acknowledges with thanks the permission granted by Mr Leonard Woolf and the Hogarth Press to quote so extensively from the works of Virginia Woolf.

CONTENTS

INTRODUCTION   *page* 7

ACKNOWLEDGMENTS   13

I   *Street Music* and *Street Haunting*   17

II   *Night and Day*   26

III *Jacob's Room*   40

IV   *Mrs Dalloway*   48

V   *Orlando* and *A Room of One's Own*   56

VI   *The Waves*   71

VII Flush's London   78

VIII *The Years:* The London Novel   83

IX   *The Years:* The Present Day   106

X   Epilogue: *A Writer's Diary*   113

INDEX   119

I

Street Music

and

Street Haunting

'London is enchanting. I step out upon a tawny coloured magic carpet, it seems, and get carried into beauty without raising a finger. The nights are amazing, with all the white porticos and broad silent avenues. And people pop in and out, lightly, divertingly like rabbits; and I look down South-ampton Row, wet as a seal's back or red and yellow with sunshine, and watch the omnibuses going and coming and hear the old crazy organs. One of these days I will write about London, and how it takes up the private life and carries it on, without any effort. Faces passing lift up my mind; prevent it from settling, as it does in the stillness at Rodmell.'

At the time of this entry in the *Diary* (May 26, 1924), Leonard and Virginia Woolf were living at 52 Tavistock Square, Bloomsbury, and she was writing *Mrs Dalloway* and finding London the right place for writing it. 'Life up-holds one; and with my squirrel cage mind it's a great thing to be stopped circling. Then to see human beings freely and quickly is an infinite gain to me. And I can dart in and out and refresh my stagnancy.' *Mrs Dalloway* is a London book, but so also is the earlier *Night and Day*, and London is one of Jacob's rooms. If one novel is more completely the London

Virginia Woolf's London

book than any other, it is *The Years*, which comes late in the series.

The fascination of London was nothing new to the London-born Virginia Stephen. As far back as 1905 she contributed an article on London Street Music to *The National Review*, a periodical devoted to very serious discussion on political, military, religious, industrial, and literary topics. If one imagines an evening forum, with speeches by distinguished authorities on the problems and obligations of Empire, being enlivened during an intermission by the music of an Italian organ-grinder or a German street band, one can appreciate the surprising effect of this little essay by Miss Virginia Stephen, following H. J. Makinder on 'Man Power as a Measure of National and Imperial Strength'. The London squares were officially inhospitable to street musicians, in the interest of peace and propriety; but the German band gave a weekly concert, and the Italian organ-grinders appeared punctually, and received coppers at the area steps which it was beneath the dignity of lovers of music to throw from the drawing-room windows. And there were violinists and vocalists, too. 'I have seen violinists who were obviously using their instruments to express something in their own hearts as they swayed by the kerb in Fleet Street . . . Indeed I once followed a disreputable old man who, with eyes shut so that he might better perceive the melodies of his soul, literally played himself from Kensington to Knightsbridge in a trance of musical ecstacy, from which a coin would have been a disagreeable awakening.'

The vagrant musicians provoke thoughts on the English suspicion of artists, whom they try to respect and domesticate if successful; and on the possibility that artists, and especially musicians, may be of divine origin, descendants of the gods who went into exile when the Christian altars arose. There may be unheard melodies in the air, accom-

panying that vast pulsation which an attentive ear can sometimes detect in forests and solitary places. But back from
speculations on rhythm and harmony to the barrel organ
in the street, which 'by reason of its crude and emphatic
rhythm, sets all the legs of the passers-by walking in time;
a band in the centre of the wild discord of cabs and carriages
would be more effectual than any policeman; not only cabman
but horse would find himself constrained to keep time to the
dance, and to follow whatever measure of trot or canter the
trumpets dictated.'

The street music that sounds again and again in Virginia
Woolf's London scenes can still be heard in the London of
today; a gypsy singing a song about her lavender in Duke
of York Street, 'Tipperary' coming from a barrel organ in
Jermyn Street, classical opera from an accordion in Russell
Square, a brass band in Oxford Street in the middle of the
'wild discord' of the buses and motor-cars that have sup-
planted the cabs and horses and carriages of 1905.

What are the advantages of observing London as a stranger?
A certain detachment and freshness, Mrs Woolf points out
in a review of two books about London by a Frenchman
and a German (1908). A Cockney has a confusing number of
echoes and sights aroused by the mention of Oxford Street,
Kensington Gardens and Piccadilly. But a foreign observer
finds 'perpetual fascination in the sight of the immense town
which has gone on growing for so many centuries, absorbing
whole worlds and finding space for them, adding impartially
splendid buildings and mean ones, and holding the tumult
together by some central heat of its own.'

A few years later, reviewing *London Revisited* by E. V.
Lucas, but almost forgetting him in her own enthusiasms, she
declares herself willing to read one volume about every street
in the City and ask for more. 'From the bones of extinct
monsters and the coins of Roman emperors in the cellars

Virginia Woolf's London

to the name of the shopman over the door, the whole story is fascinating and the material endless. Perhaps Cockneys are a prejudiced race, but certainly this inexhaustible richness seems to belong to London more than to any other great city . . . But each Londoner has a London in his mind which is the real London, some denying the right of Bayswater to be included, others of Kensington, and each feels for London as he feels for his family, quietly but deeply, and with a quick eye for affront.' She is not uncritical, and regrets some of the recent rebuilding, deploring the lavish use of white stone (which Lucas admires), because it lends itself in the hands of modern architects to wedding-cake decorations of scrolls and festoons. But even the white stone can be beautiful; in the last two winters, with the lights dimmed by wartime regulations, 'many of us must have realized the beauty of the white church spires for the first time; as they lie against the blue of the night in their ethereal ghostliness.' She does not admire the mounds of statuary placed at the wrongs spots, nor does she appreciate the open-air statues as Lucas does, 'but even the statues of London are lovable; and sparrows find the top hats of statesmen good lodging places for their nests.' One piece of sculpture that is pleasing to the eye is the statue of a woman with an urn at the entrance to the Foundling Hospital. And how many new facts one is always picking up as one walks the streets! Marvell, Chapman, James Shirley, and Lord Herbert of Cherbury are buried in St Giles-in-the-Fields off Charing Cross Road; and the lamp-posts in the parish of St Martin-in-the-Fields bear a relief of St Martin giving his cloak to the beggar.

A long habit of strolling and looking must have provided these delightful but incidental observations on London. Finally—and after many of her own characters had been walking to good purpose—Mrs Woolf wrote a single essay that epitomizes the pleasures of street haunting. This essay

Street Music and Street Haunting

is a key to the fascination exercised by London on her imagination as a novelist. *Street Haunting: a London Adventure* was first published in the *Yale Review* (1927). Rambling the streets of London, she writes, is the greatest pleasure of town life in winter, and the best time is between four and six, when darkness and lamp-light bestow irresponsibility. When we go out and shut the door, we shed the self our friends know us by and leave behind the objects which 'perpetually express the oddity of our own temperaments', and become one of the army of anonymous trampers. 'The shell-like covering which our souls have excreted to house themselves, to make for themselves a shape distinct from others, is broken, and there is left of all these wrinkles and roughnesses a central oyster of perceptiveness, an enormous eye . . . The eye is not a miner, not a diver, not a seeker after buried treasure. It floats us smoothly down a stream; resting, pausing, the brain sleeps perhaps as it looks.'

The London street is beautiful at this hour, with its islands of light and long groves of darkness; and here are the grass-grown spaces of a square that holds the country in it—a square 'set about by offices and houses where at this hour fierce lights burn over maps, over documents, over desks where clerks sit turning with wetted forefinger the files of endless correspondences; or more suffusedly the firelight wavers and the lamplight falls upon the privacy of some drawing-room, its easy chairs, its papers, its china, its inlaid table, and the figure of a woman, accurately measuring out the precise number of spoons of tea which—she looks at the door as if she heard a ring downstairs . . . ' The square might be Tavistock Square, where Virginia Woolf was living at this time, or Russell Square, past which she would walk down Southampton Row on her way to the Strand. And the odd mingling of drawing-rooms and tea with offices and clerks has a precision reflecting the changes the early 19th century houses in Bloomsbury were undergoing, from residences to apartments, offices and boarding-houses.

But the rambler who is Virginia Woolf realizes that, in imagining a drawing-room scene, she is digging deeper than the eye approves, yielding to a temptation which her Bernard, in *The Waves*, the novel she was beginning to work on, is always exposed to—the temptation to stir up memories, to invent stories. So she enters a boot shop and becomes interested in a customer, a dwarf with beautiful feet and great pride in them, and watches the little scene played out between the dwarf, her companions and the saleswoman. The dwarf has so changed her mood that, on returning to the street, she notices the grotesque and the maimed, the halt and the blind; 'the dwarf had started a hobbling grotesque dance to which everybody in the street now conformed.' Where did they all live? Some perhaps in the top rooms of 'those narrow old houses between Holborn and Soho, where people have such queer names, and pursue so many curious trades.' Her thoughts shift to the derelicts one often sees lying not a stone's throw from the theatres, almost within touch of the 'sequined cloaks and bright legs of diners and dancers'; or close to shop windows, offering to these old women laid on doorsteps, or blind men or hobbling dwarfs, sofas 'supported by the gilt necks of proud swans, tables inlaid with many-coloured fruits.' The window of an antique dealer, with its jewels, calls up a fanciful picture of Mayfair streets late in the evening, with peers, silk-stockinged footmen, dowagers and prime ministers—and a cat creeping along a garden wall. But it isn't midnight in Mayfair, but six o'clock on a winter's evening. The second-hand bookshops in Charing Cross Road interrupt a revery on the nature of the true self, and start another on the world of books, allusive and suggestive. Out in the streets again, the rambler mingles with the crowd on its way home from work, and overhears tantalizing scraps of conversation, affording glimpses into many lives. 'Dreaming, gesticulating, often muttering a few words aloud, they sweep over the Strand and across Waterloo Bridge, whence they will be slung in long rattling trains, to some prim little villa in Barnes or Surbiton.'

With the sight of the Thames comes a memory of leaning over the Embankment wall on a summer evening. (And how many of Virginia Woolf's characters lean over that wall!) But the winter river is rough and grey and the tide is running out to sea and a tug and two barges are going down with the tide, and a couple, lovers perhaps, are leaning over the balustrade. The street-haunter must go back to the Strand and buy a pencil at a stationer's shop. A little half-story is suggested by the stationer and his wife, who seem to have been quarrelling, but who have forgotten their quarrel by the time the box of pencils has been found and one chosen.

And now the streets are empty. 'Life had withdrawn to the top floor, and lamps were lit. The pavement was dry and hard; the road was of hammered silver. Walking home through the desolation one could tell oneself the story of the dwarf, of the blind men, of the party in the Mayfair mansion, of the quarrel in the stationer's shop. Into each of these lives one could penetrate a little way, far enough to give oneself the illusion that one is not tethered to a single mind, but can put on briefly the bodies and minds of others. One could become a washerwoman, a publican, a street singer. And what greater delight and wonder can there be than to leave the straight lines of personality and deviate into those footpaths that lead beneath brambles and thick tree trunks into the heart of the forest where live those wild beasts, our fellowmen.' And now the self is back in its sheltered place among its own possessions, this self 'which has been blown about at so many street-corners, which has battered like a moth at the flame of so many inaccessible lanterns.'

Virginia Woolf's London

The road of hammered silver, the cat creeping along the garden wall, the barges going down with the tide, the nameless crowds sweeping across Waterloo Bridge—lovers of Virginia Woolf's novels will recognise these and other scenes and phrases that found their place in her later work. Like Henry James, another street haunter, she walked not only for exercise and amusement but for 'acquisition'. To a curious mind like his, this practice of walking provoked a 'mystic solicitation' on the part of everything to be interpreted; the common air 'tasted' of subjects and situations, character and history. To both artists the London streets offered a 'thick tribute'. It is in the preface to *The Princess Casamassima* that James states that the novel proceeded quite directly from his habit of walking the streets during the first year of his long residence in London. Reviewing James's *Letters* in the *Times Literary Supplement* (April 8, 1920), Mrs Woolf noted that London 'exercised a continuous double pressure of attraction and repulsion to which he finally succumbed, to the extent of making his headquarters in the metropolis without shutting his eyes to her faults. "I am attracted to London in spite of the long list of reasons why I should not be; I think it, on the whole, the best point of view in the world." ' Further on in the review she comments with a shade of disapproval on James's attitude: 'If London is primarily a point of view, if the whole field of human activity is only a prospect and a pageant, then we cannot help asking, as the store of impressions heaps itself up, what is the aim of the spectator, what is the purpose of his hoard? A spectator, alert, aloof, endlessly interested, endlessly observant, Henry James undoubtedly was.' Yet, in the *Letters* at least, she finds no clue to the purpose of the hoard of London impressions. She was obviously irritated by the tone of detachment and condescension in James's phrase about London as 'on the whole', with all her faults, 'the best point of view in the world'. She herself was quite as endlessly interested and endlessly observant as James. But London was not a point of view to the born Londoner, to be selected from among other points of view after due consideration. Writing about her father, Sir Leslie Stephen, on the centenary of his birth, she recalls how he would take his hat and his stick, and 'calling for his dog and his daughter, he would stride off into Kensington Gardens, where he had walked as a little boy, where his brother Fitzjames and he had made beautiful bows to young Queen Victoria and she had swept them a curtesy, and so, round the Serpentine, to Hyde Park Corner, where he had once saluted the great Duke himself; and so home. He was not then in the least "alarming"; he was very simple, very confiding; and his silence, though one might last unbroken from the Round Pond to the Marble Arch, was curiously full of meaning, as if he were thinking half aloud, about poetry and philosophy and people he had known.'

Henry James, like Virginia Woolf, had a father who 'cultivated the company' of his little boy; took him walking along Broadway or sailing on summer afternoons from Manhattan to Fort Hamilton. The small boy dreamed of the places his parents talked about—Piccadilly, the Green Park, Richmond —but it was Fourteenth Street that he 'realised' at a very tender age. There is no grudging 'on the whole' in his appreciation of the quiet harmonies of Washington Square. But however one defines the special charm London held for each of these artists, they both, in James's words, plucked from her streets 'the ripe round fruit of perambulation', and heard the deep notes thrown out from 'their vast vague murmur'.

II

Night and Day

To what purpose did Virginia Woolf put her hoard of London impressions? We can ask that of her as she asked it of Henry James. But her first novel is not the place to look for an answer, since London is merely the port of departure for the characters in *The Voyage Out*. We first meet two of them, Mr and Mrs Ambrose, on the Embankment near Waterloo Bridge, pausing to look at the river before taking a cab to the docks. Mrs Ambrose, sad at leaving her children to go on the long cruise to South America, leans her elbows on the balustrade and weeps, while Mr Ambrose walks up and down, reciting scraps of poetry and flourishing his stick at some intruding little boys. 'Someone,' comments Mrs Woolf, 'is always looking into the river near Waterloo Bridge; a couple will stand there talking for half an hour on a fine afternoon; most people, walking for pleasure, contemplate for three minutes . . . Sometimes the flats and churches and hotels of Westminster are like the outlines of Constantinople in a mist; sometimes the river is an opulent purple, sometimes mud-coloured, sometimes sparkling blue like the sea. It is always worth while to look down and see what is happening.' But not worth while for Mrs Ambrose, who sees through her tears only a 'circular iridescent patch slowly floating past with a straw in the middle of it'. Mr Ambrose tries to console her; she wipes her eyes and raises them to the level of the factory chimneys on the other bank, sees the arches of the bridge and the carts moving across them, 'like the line of animals in a shooting gallery'. In her sad mood she sees London only as a place that has done little to make her love it.

On the drive from the West End to the East End and the docks, as the rich give place to the workers, she is further depressed by the innumerable poor. It seems to occur to her for the first time that it is the ordinary thing to be poor, and she is startled into seeing herself pacing a circle all the days of her life round Piccadilly Circus. Rescued by an old boat-man from the teeming activity of waggons and sacks and the smells of malt and oil, they set out in his little boat to board the steamer. 'The river, which had a certain amount of troubled light in it, ran with great force; bulky barges floated down swiftly escorted by tugs; police boats shot past every-thing; the wind went with the current. The open rowing-boat in which they sat bobbed and curtseyed across the line of traffic.' The old man resting on his oars a moment recalled earlier days when he had many passengers, but they all wanted bridges now, he said, indicating 'the monstrous outline of the Tower Bridge'.

They board the steamer and the voyage begins. 'They were now moving steadily down the river, passing the dark shapes of ships at anchor, and London was a swarm of lights with a pale yellow canopy drooping above it. There were the lights of the great theatres, the lights of the long streets, lights which indicated huge squares of domestic comfort, lights that hung high in air. No darkness would ever settle upon those lamps, as no darkness had settled upon them for hundreds of years. It seemed dreadful that the town should blaze for ever in the same spot; dreadful at least to people going away to adventure upon the sea, and beholding it as a circumscribed mound, eternally burnt, eternally scarred. From the deck of the ship the great city appeared a crouched and cowardly figure, a sedentary miser.'

Virginia Woolf's London

This impression, coloured by Mrs Ambrose's sad mood, recalls the prelude to Conrad's *Heart of Darkness*, where Marlow and his friends, on the deck of a yawl anchored in the river waiting for the tide, look towards London and the shore and then out towards 'the heart of darkness' in Africa; and Marlow reflects that the site of London was once, too, one of the dark places of the earth. 'Dusk fell on the stream, and lights began to appear along the shore . . . Lights of ships moved in the fairway—a great stir of light going up and going down. And further west on the upper reaches the place of the monstrous town was still marked ominously on the sky, a brooding gloom in sunshine, a lurid glare under the stars.'

The phrase 'heart of darkness' recurs a number of times in Virginia Woolf's work, sometimes standing as a kind of symbol of prehistoric London. People toil 'in the heart of darkness, in the depths of night'; 'in the middle of the jungle, in the heart of darkness'; lovers have always fought as the dog fights the vixen, 'in the heart of darkness, in the fields of night'. The site of London as once one of the dark places of the earth fascinates old Mrs Swithin, in *Between the Acts*, reading her Outline of History, and thinking of rhododendron forests in Piccadilly and of all sorts of elephant-bodied, seal-necked monsters. And the ancient song of love sung by the old street-singer in *Mrs Dalloway* had been bubbling up like a spring through all the ages, even when the pavement had been swamp, in the age of tusk and mammoth.

Though it is in South America where Rachel falls in love with Terence, it is London where they plan to live. London's the place, says Terence. 'They looked together at the carpet, as though London itself were to be seen there lying on the floor, with all its spires and pinnacles pricking through the smoke . . . "On the whole what I should like best at this moment," Terence pondered, "would be to find myself walking down Kingsway, by those big placards, you know, and turning into the Strand. Perhaps I might go and look over Waterloo Bridge for a moment. Then I'd go along the Strand past the shops with all the new books in them, and through the little archway into the Temple. I always like the quiet after the uproar. You hear your own footsteps suddenly quite loud. The Temple's very pleasant. I think I should go and see if I could find dear old Hodgkin—the man who writes books about Van Eyck, you know. When I left England he was very sad about his tame magpie. He suspected that a maid had poisoned it. And then Russell lives on the next stair-case. I think you'd like him. He's a passion for Handel. Well, Rachel," he concluded, dismissing the vision of London, "we shall be doing that together in six weeks' time, and it'll be the middle of June then,—and June in London—my God, how pleasant it all is!" '

But Rachel dies in South America, and it is Clarissa Dalloway who enjoys London in June, and the lovers in *Night and Day* who take the London walks dreamed of by Terence.

These lovers—Katharine Hilbery, Mary Datchet, Cassandra Otway, William Rodney, and Ralph Denham—work out their emotional maladjustments and marital solutions during a few months in London, with an interlude in Lincolnshire. There are London interiors: the Hilbery home in Cheyne Walk, Chelsea, with its social amenities and traditional intellectual values; the crowded friendly middle-class home of the Denhams in Highgate; Rodney's rooms in the Temple; Mary's rooms off the Strand and her office in Russell Square; and Ralph's office in Lincoln's Inn. The story moves at a livelier pace when it takes to the streets and the parks; the Strand, the Embankment, Charing Cross Road, Kingsway, Southampton Row, Regent's Park, and, further afield, Kew Gardens, Greenwich, Hampton Court. The young people walk a great deal, alone or in pairs or even foursomes, in planned or accidental conjunctions; they ride in taxi (rarely) or in buses, preferably on top in the front seats. They lean on the Embankment balustrade and watch the Thames run softly or roughly.

Katharine and Ralph, strolling in Kew Gardens on a spring day, seeking for terms on which they can build a friendship, come to a pause; and Katharine, walking on beneath the beech trees and swinging her umbrella, meditates, 'Why should there be this perpetual disparity between the thought and the action, between the life of solitude and the life of society, this astonishing precipice on one side of which the soul was active and in broad daylight, on the other side of which it was contemplative and dark as night? Was it not possible to step from one to the other, erect and without essential change?' They have tea, wander in and out of the glass-houses, look at lilies swimming in tanks, breathe in the scent of carnations, and while talking exclusively of what they saw, 'they felt that the compact between them was made firmer and deeper by the number of people who passed them and suspected nothing of the kind'. The *night* is the inner, the *day* the outer, in the perpetual interplay between the self and its environment. To bring inner and outer into harmony is the aim of many of Virginia Woolf's experiments in technique; and this harmony, when achieved at rare moments, is the perfect flowing together of the stream of consciousness and the stream of events. It is symbolized by one of her favourite images, that of the globe, which 'we spend our lives trying to shape, round, whole and entire from the confusion of chaos'.

London, as *Street Haunting* makes clear, is a rich source of the outer stream, and by the time Mrs Woolf wrote *Night and Day*, she was ready to use London in several ways. As the physical setting, of course, where people live and work out their destinies; and she often sets the scene in brief objective descriptions in the traditional manner of fiction. Now and then outer details and inner mood are blended in the Hardy manner, to make us see and feel with the character; as when Katharine finds the streets of South Kensington inexpressibly dreary, when her mood is sad and chastened. But to escape is the greatest of the pleasures London offers, not escape as evasion, but as release—that release into the general life which the street haunter experienced.

Several of the characters in *Night and Day* are street haunters, or become so as their emotional difficulties grow acute. Katharine, who being of the privileged thinks more of taking taxis than of walking, finds herself as she tries to adjust her complicated relations with her two suitors taking long walks and bus rides. Somewhat depressed by a glimpse, in Mary's office in Russell Square, of the world of typewriters and Causes, she goes out with Ralph and is so exhilarated by 'the crowded street, with its pendant necklace of lamps, its lighted windows, and its throng of men and women' that she almost forgets her companion. An earlier walk with Ralph along the Embankment has almost the same effect. Ralph feels he must explain his feelings, explain his family, explain his life; and they walk on and on, and Ralph talks on and on, and Katharine listens attentively enough to pass an examination by the time Waterloo Bridge is in sight. But a kind of vague happiness, without reason, pervades her, and her mind turns to a certain secret, disinterested concern of hers—mathematics; 'If Denham could have seen how visibly books of algebraic symbols, pages all speckled with dots and dashes and twisted bars, came before her eyes as they trod the Embankment, his secret joy in her attention might have been dispersed . . . All the time she was in fancy looking up through a telescope at white shadow-cleft discs which were other worlds, until she felt herself possessed of two bodies, one walking by the river with Denham, the other concentrated to a silver globe aloft in the fine blue space above the scum of vapours that was covering the visible world.' She is released into something impersonal, both by the love she is becoming aware of and by the walk through the London night by the river.

During a late crisis in Katharine's devious love affair with Ralph, she seeks him at his office but it is late and she misses him; and at this point she is completely absorbed in her own anxiety. Leaving Lincoln's Inn Fields, she turns into the great torrent of vans and carts and pedestrians that was sweeping down Kingsway, and stands fascinated at the corner. 'The deep roar filled her ears; the changing tumult had the inexpressible fascination of varied life pouring ceaselessly with a purpose which, as she looked, seemed to her, somehow, the normal purpose for which life was framed; its complete indifference to the individuals, whom it swallowed up and rolled onwards, filled her with at least a temporary exaltation. The blend of daylight and of lamplight made her an invisible spectator, just as it gave the people who passed her a semi-transparent quality, and left the faces pale ivory ovals in which the eyes alone were dark. They tended the enormous rush of the current—the great flow, the deep stream, the unquenchable tide.' Continuing to seek Ralph, Katharine covers much ground before she finds him, many pages, streets and taxis later, at her home in Cheyne Walk, and falls at last into his arms.

Bus-riding seems to promote understanding between Ralph and Katharine, whose temperaments are difficult and ideals exigent. One night they ride on top of a bus from Chelsea to Temple Bar. 'After curving through streets of comparative darkness, so narrow that shadows on the blinds were pressed within a few feet of their faces, they came to one of those great knots of activity where the lights, having drawn close together, thin out again and take their separate ways. They were borne on until they saw the spires of the city churches pale and flat against the sky.' They alight at Temple Bar, and 'the splendid race of lights drawn past her eyes by the superb swerving and curving of the monster on which she sat was at an end. They had followed some such course in their thoughts, too'. They walk on, pausing outside Mary's lighted windows to look up, and again boarding an omnibus, they ride through almost empty streets. 'No longer did the shadow of a man sing to the shadow of a piano. A few lights in bedroom windows burnt but were extinguished one by one as the omnibus passed them.' Dismounting, they walked down to the river and looked at the dark tide of waters, endlessly moving, beneath them. They were together in spirit.

There is, as the reviewer of the novel in the *Times Literary Supplement* pointed out, a geographical significance in this love affair: 'In the end of it, Highgate has come to Chelsea; raw strength to exquisite tradition.'

To Rodney, Katharine's unsuccessful suitor, London means much; as he points out to her the view from the window of his rooms in a high eighteenth century house, towards the City, he says, 'I couldn't live without this.' The City wore at that moment 'the appearance of a town cut out of grey-blue cardboard, and pasted flat against the sky, which was of a deeper blue.' One of his windows looks out upon a courtyard with flagged pavement and a single tree, and across to 'the flat red-brick fronts of the opposite houses, which would not have surprised Dr Johnson, if he had come out of his grave for a turn in the moonlight'. (As later, in *Orlando*, he does, along with other London ghosts). There is much looking out of windows in *Night and Day*, sometimes mere stage business but at other times significant as a movement of eye and mind from the inner world to the outer. A good part of Katharine's life is passed doing duty in the drawing-room or working with her mother on her father's memoirs. The sounds of London come into her mother's room; straining her ears, she could just hear, far off, 'the hoot of a motor-car and the

rush of wheels coming nearer and dying away again, and the
voices of men crying old iron and vegetables in one of the
poorer streets at the back of the house'. In the drawing-room,
full of people, she takes a moment off to push aside the blind
and look out at the river—a dark night, the water barely
visible, cabs passing, couples loitering along the road; and
she determines to forget individual lives and wishes she could
drive through the streets, alone.

Ralph, the champion walker in this novel, is not always alert
to his surroundings. Absorbed in his own thoughts, he is more
irritated than not by chance encounters. One night he calls
upon Rodney in his rooms in the Temple, but finding him
out, he starts to walk in the direction of Chelsea—and
Katharine. It is Sunday, and he has already tramped 'both
far and fast'. As he rests for a bit on a bench along the Embankment, an elderly derelict sits down beside him, begs a
match and tells a tale of woe; and Ralph has an impulse to
talk about his own troubles (for Katharine is, he thinks, about
to marry Rodney). The old man's ancient story of ill luck and
undeserved misfortune goes down the wind in an unhappy
voice that at first saddens Ralph and then almost angers him.
He thinks of a lighthouse 'besieged by the flying bodies of
lost birds, who were dashed senseless by the gale, against the
glass. He had a strange sensation that he was both lighthouse
and bird; he was steadfast and brilliant; and at the same time
he was whirled, with all other things, senseless against the
glass'. The image persists as he walks on past the Houses of
Parliament and down Grosvenor Road by the side of the river.
Finally reaching the Hilberys' house, he stands across the
street leaning against the Embankment balustrade, looks at
the three long lighted windows of the drawing-room, imagines
what is going on inside, and seems to see Katharine as a shape
of light, the light itself; and he seemed, 'simplified and
exhausted as he was, to be like one of those lost birds fascin-

ated by the lighthouse and held to the glass by the splendour
of the blaze'.

Ralph's self-absorption is so complete that when during
his lunch hour he sits on a bench in Lincoln's Inn Fields and
feeds the sparrows, he might as well be sitting in his room.
Even London cannot tempt him to look outward so long as
he is in the grip of his unhappy emotions and indecisions.
Mary Datchet, who is falling in love with him, sees him there
and touches him on the shoulder, and they talk, while the
sparrows flutter about the crumbs and a child, rolling a hoop,
breaks into the group of birds and prevents a bald, nearly
tame cock-sparrow from settling on Ralph's arm.

Mary becomes later on almost as self-absorbed as Ralph,
with the growing realization of the hopelessness of her love,
and loses the mood of exhilaration at being in the centre of
the wonderful maze of London, which seemed to her like
'a vast electric light, casting radiance upon the myriads of
men and women who crowded round it'. When at night in her
rooms off the Strand she hears the strokes of Big Ben, it is
a message from Westminster itself. (Big Ben and Ralph's
lighthouse image, incidental in this novel, become integral
in the symbolism of *Mrs Dalloway* and *To the Lighthouse*).
Mary likes to be on the streets with the crowds of workers at
morning rush hours, between the Strand and Russell Square;
likes to think herself indistinguishable from the rest; likes even,
when driven by rain into the Underground or a bus, to take
her share of crowd and wet with the clerks and typists and
commercial men, and share 'the serious business of winding
up the world to tick for another four-and-twenty hours'.
Walking up Kingsway and through Southampton Row to
Russell Square, she pauses now and then to look into the
window of some book or flower shop, noticing the still empty
gaps in the display of goods, feeling kindly disposed towards
the shopkeepers and hoping they would trick the midday

public into purchases. She thinks of her own work, of note-paper and foolscap, and the great job of that radical reconstruction of society which she and her fellow-workers were determined to bring about. And so she climbs to her desk at the top of the old house in Russell Square, once lived in by a great merchant and his family.

But this nice adjustment is threatened by her growing love for Ralph. Once she turns off into the British Museum before going to her office, and finds a bench directly beneath the gaze of the Elgin marbles. As usual, looking at them, she feels exalted; but as Mrs Woolf explains—something she would not dream of doing later on—her emotions were not purely aesthetic, for she begins to think about Ralph. 'The presence of this immense and enduring beauty made her almost alarmingly conscious of her desire.' Moving on to the engraved obelisks and the winged Assyrian bulls, her emotions take another flight, travelling with Ralph to a land where these monsters were 'couchant in the sand'.

It is Mary's fate to be the 'odd woman out' in the group of five. She has to build alone a future beyond her frustration, and her bleak triumph is largely achieved with the aid of the London streets and the thoughts that are stirred by her walks. These thoughts and speculations are presented for the most part in analytical explanatory way that Mrs Woolf soon abandoned for the technique that reached perfection in *Mrs Dalloway*. As Mary's unhappiness grows, she begins to feel, even as she competently does her day's work, like a hollow machine. Walking down Charing Cross Road to lunch at a shop in the Strand, she considered her case. Would she mind being crushed under the wheels of that omnibus? The light in the eyes of the young women looking into the milliners' windows, the eagerness in the eyes of the elderly men turning over books in the secondhand bookshops—she lacked that, caring neither for clothes, money, nor even books, which were

too closely connected with Ralph. She felt completely alien
to the crowds through which she pushed her way. Then her
mood changes. 'Strange thoughts are bred in passing through
crowded streets should the passenger, by chance, have no
exact destination in front of him, much as the mind shapes
all kinds of forms, solutions, images, when listening attentively
to music. From an acute consciousness of herself as an individual, Mary passed to a conception of the scheme of things in
which, as a human being, she must have her share.' Half
seeing a vision, she wished she had a pencil and paper to
give it a form as she walked on down Charing Cross Road.
The vision seemed to lay out the lines of her life till death.
'It only needed a persistent effort of thought, stimulated in this
strange way by the crowd and the noise, to climb the crest of
existence and see it all laid out once and for ever. Already her
suffering as an individual was left behind her.' Only two
articulate words escaped her—'not happiness'. And she spoke
them aloud as she sat down for a moment opposite the statue
of one of London's heroes on the Embankment.

But the exalted mood breaks up when she thinks of Ralph,
with something like hatred for his cruelty. And now comes a
passage mingling the outer and the inner flow, with a promise
of Virginia Woolf's later brilliance. ' "But I refuse—I refuse
to hate anyone," she said aloud; chose the moment to cross
the road with circumspection, and ten minutes later lunched
in the Strand, cutting her meat firmly into small pieces, but
giving her fellow diners no further cause to judge her eccentric.
Her soliloquy crystallized itself into little fragmentary phrases
emerging suddenly from the turbulence of her thought,
particularly when she had to exert herself in any way, either to
move, to count money, or to choose a turning. "To know
the truth—to accept without bitterness"—these, perhaps,
were the most articulate of her utterances, for no one could
have made head or tail of the queer gibberish murmured in

front of the statue of Francis, Duke of Bedford . . .' So
we leave Mary. (And we can find Francis, Duke of Bedford,
in Russell Square).

Cassandra Otway feels the fascination of London while
on a visit with her cousins, the Hilberys, during which she
gets engaged to Rodney, happily relinquished by Katharine.
Her walk along Bond Street in the spring gives us a foretaste
of Mrs Dalloway's excursion to buy flowers for her party.
In the florists' windows are 'buds that open and flowers that
suddenly shake their petals—white, purple, or crimson—in
competition with the display in the garden beds, although
these city flowers are merely so many doors flung wide in
Bond Street and the neighbourhood, inviting you to look at
a picture or hear a symphony, or merely crowd and rush
yourself among all sorts of vocal, excitable, brightly coloured
human beings'.

London is surrounded by pleasant places, adapted admirably 'to the needs of people between the ages of twenty
and thirty with Saturday afternoons to spend,'—among them
Kew Gardens, Hampton Court and Greenwich. Kew Gardens,
says Ralph to Katharine, after he had failed to explain himself in the walk along the Embankment, is 'the only place to
discuss things satisfactorily that I know of'. She agrees. In
a pleasant little walk-and-conversation scene, they move a step
nearer to understanding, among the green spaces, the tree
vistas, with the spring air stirring, 'the ruffled gold of the
Thames in the distance and the Ducal castle standing in its
meadows', and almost nobody around. Ralph uncovers with
his stick little plants and leaves and gives Katharine (ignorant
of botany) some valuable information about English trees
and plants. But Katharine among the orchids in the Orchid
House disturbs the calm that came to him in talking of his
hobby. Her beauty was so emphasized by the fantastic plants
that he found his ardour for botany waning and more complex

feelings taking hold.

All four happy lovers come to Hampton Court on the third day of a prolonged holiday which they are enjoying, about lunchtime on a fine Sunday morning. They walk up and down the Terrace four abreast, and everything is in a benignant state, including the deer and the fish. Part of the pleasure in following Virginia Woolf's London pattern comes from noting how in one book a scene is a mere sketch, in another a fully pictured background, and in another that same street or square or garden is a major influence in the solution of human problems. New techniques produce new effects. The Hampton Court of *The Waves* is no mere pleasant spot for an afternoon's outing; it lies under a spell. *Kew Gardens*, the impressionistic piece published in the same year as *Night and Day*, marks a significant point in Virginia Woolf's development. She was 'breaking the mould', and without the experimentation in this sketch and in *The Mark on the Wall* (also published in 1919) there would have been no *Jacob's Room* and *Mrs Dalloway*. Clive Bell, in *Old Friends*, makes no effort at analysis of *Kew Gardens*, but writes: 'We are familiar with the way in which Renoir and Monet proclaim their sense of a garden blazing in the sun. It is something that comes to them in colours and shapes, and in shapes and colours must be rendered. Now see how an artist in words deals with a like experience.' Then he quotes the passage beginning, 'How hot it was!' and ending, 'But there was no silence; all the time the motor onmibuses were turning their wheels and changing their gear; like a vast nest of Chinese boxes, all of wrought steel turning ceaselessly one within another, the city murmured; on the top of which the voices cried aloud and the petals of myriads of flowers flashed their colours into the air.'

III

Jacob's Room

Was the technique of *Kew Gardens* evidence that Virginia Woolf had discovered the cinema? To quote Winifred Holtby, 'To let the perspective shift from high to low, from huge to microscopic, to let people, insects, aeroplanes, flowers pass across the vision and melt away'—these are the devices of the cinema. Some of them are used in *Jacob's Room*, the story of one of the thousands of young men killed in the 1914-1918 war. What was lost when such a young man was killed, what did he himself lose, and what sense of loss and sorrow is in the cry of Jacob's friend at the end—Jacob, Jacob!—in the emptiness of Jacob's room?

London is only one of Jacob's rooms and shares our interest with Scarborough, Cambridge, Cornwall, Paris and Greece. Though Jacob moves in and out of the London scenes and is presumably influenced by them and once in a while expresses pleasure or disgust, it is the places rather than the young man that one remembers. It is Waterloo Bridge with the throngs of people incessantly passing back and forth; the loaded barges in the river; Oxford Street in a traffic jam; the sordid streets of Soho on a rainy autumn night; the dim interior of St Paul's; the swarms of office workers pouring into the Underground; the boisterous crowd around a Guy Fawkes bonfire on Parliament Hill; the banners of a demonstration glittering down Whitehall; Hyde Park on a hot summer afternoon; the readers under the dome of the British Museum,

and, late at night, its immense mound sleek in the rain.

After his childhood in Scarborough and his college years at
Cambridge, Jacob comes to London and lives in rooms rather
vaguely located near Lamb's Conduit Street in Bloomsbury,
going daily to an office in the City, riding on buses along
Oxford Street, sitting in Hyde Park, drifting in and out of
St Paul's, walking and dining in Soho with Florinda, reading
in the British Museum, and going to teas, dinners and dances
in very good society. If the omnibus is stalled in the traffic
on Oxford Street, we assume that the October sunlight rests
on Jacob as on the other passengers, who are picked out with
the camera for an instant and then vanish for ever. But the
impression of what it is like to be on the bus, halted and
jerked on again, is indelible: 'Oh yes, human life is very
tolerable on the top of an omnibus in Holborn, when the
policeman holds up his arm and the sun beats on your back,
and if there is such a thing as a shell secreted by man to fit man
himself here we find it, on the banks of the Thames, where
the great streets join and St Paul's Cathedral, like the volute
on top of the snail shell, finishes it off.'

Jacob, alighting from the bus at St Paul's, consults his watch
and decides to go in. What he sees or thinks or feels while he
is there, we do not learn. Perhaps he sees Mrs Lidgett, seated
beneath the great Duke's tomb, with folded hands and half-
closed eyes: 'a magnificent place for an old woman to rest in,
by the very side of the great Duke's bones, whose victories
mean nothing to her, whose name she knows not, though
she never fails to greet the little angels opposite, as she passes
out, wishing the like on her own tomb, for the leathern curtain
of the heart has flapped wide, and out steal on tiptoe thoughts
of rest, sweet melodies . . . ' Dim it is in St Paul's, 'haunted
by ghosts of white marble, to whom the organ for ever chants.'
Jacob, coming out and standing on the steps, is the only one
of the multitudes round about who will read a certain book

by his fireside that night. Thus Mrs Woolf singles him out, but deserts him instantly, to swing her camera over the crowds to whom the streets belong, and the shops and churches and desks; 'the vans are theirs, and the railway slung high above the street . . . The posters are theirs too; and the news on them . . . A homeless people, circling beneath the sky whose blue or white is held off by a ceiling cloth of steel filings and horse dung shredded to dust.' The camera picks up a woman standing against the wall, staring at nothing, bootlaces extended in her hand, which she does not ask you to buy.

If we worry about where Jacob is, we are not yet at ease with Mrs Woolf's method. Let us watch the crowds, as perhaps he is doing, coming from the nearby offices. 'Innumerable overcoats of the quality prescribed hung empty all day in the corridors, but as the clock struck six each was exactly filled, and the little figures, split apart into trousers or moulded into a single thickness, jerked rapidly with angular forward motion along the pavement; then dropped into darkness. Beneath the pavement, sunk in the earth, hollow drains lined with yellow light for ever conveyed them this way and that, and large letters upon enamel plates represented in the underworld the parks, squares and circuses of the upper . . . Home they went. The grey church spires received them; the hoary city, old, sinful, majestic. One behind another, round or pointed, piercing the sky or massing themselves, like sailing ships, like granite cliffs, spires, offices, wharves and factories crowd the bank; eternally the pilgrims trudge; barges rest in midstream heavy laden; as some believe, the city loves her prostitutes.'

At this point Jacob apparently goes to the opera. At least Clara Durant, who is there, thinks about him and perhaps sees him. But the opera is less interesting than the crowds crossing Waterloo Bridge with the stream of carts and

omnibuses and lorries. Sometimes a lorry has great forest trees chained to it; and here comes a mason's van, 'with newly lettered tombstones recording how some one loved someone who is buried at Putney'. The people never cease passing from the Surrey side to the Strand and from the Strand to the Surrey side. The river races beneath the bridge, the wind blows up the waves, and 'the men standing on the barges have to lean all their weight on the tiller'. 'St Paul's swells white above the fretted, pointed, or oblong buildings beside it. The cross alone shines rosy-gilt. But what century have we reached? Has this procession from the Surrey side to the Strand gone on for ever? That old man has been crossing the Bridge these six hundred years, with the rabble of little boys at his heels, for he is drunk, or blind with misery, and tied round with old clouts of clothing such as pilgrims might have worn. He shuffles on. No one stands still. It seems as if we marched to the sound of music; perhaps the wind and the river; perhaps these same drums and trumpets—the ecstasy and hubbub of the soul.'

In the phrase 'these six hundred years', suggesting a London enduring through the centuries, one sees emerging the idea, which finds its fantasy fulfilment in *Orlando*, and a dramatic expression in *Between the Acts;* and which was brushed lightly by Dr Johnson's ghost, evoked in *Night and Day*. A ghost or two slips from the eighteenth century into *Jacob's Room* —ghosts of the great people who lived in the old house where Jacob has his rooms; they stood, coming back from Court past midnight, 'huddling their satin skirts, under the carved door-posts while the footman roused himself from his mattress on the floor, hurriedly fastened the lower buttons of his waistcoat and let them in. The bitter eighteenth century rain rushed down the kennel.' London blazed at night even then, the lamps upholding the dark 'as upon the points of burning bayonets . . . Passengers in the mail-coaches running into London in the eighteenth century looked through leafless branches and saw it flaring beneath them.'

The old city is sinful as well as majestic. Here is Soho: the street market fierce with light; 'raw meat, china mugs, and silk stockings blaze in it'; raw voices, flaming gas-jets, people with arms akimbo, standing on the pavement, bawling; shawled women carrying babies with purple eyelids. 'Every face, every shop, bedroom window, public-house, and dark square is a picture feverishly turned—in search of what?' Jacob and Florinda, the little prostitute he had picked up around the Guy Fawkes bonfire, sit at a little restaurant table, talk, listen to others talking, and overhear a quarrel at the next table, which ends with the woman dashing plates to the floor. They go out into the wet November night where the lamps made 'large greasy spots of light upon the pavement', and where the by-streets were dark enough to shelter man or woman leaning against the doorways. Where had the angry woman of the restaurant got to? 'The street lamps do not carry far enough to tell us. The voices, angry, lustful, despairing, passionate, were scarcely more than the voices of caged beasts at night. Only they are not caged, nor beasts. Stop a man; ask him the way; he'll tell it you; but one's afraid to ask him the way. What does one fear?—the human eye. At once the pavement narrows, the chasm deepens. There! They've melted into it—both man and woman . . . And so on again into the dark, passing a girl here for sale, or there an old woman with only matches to offer, passing the crowd from the Tube station, the women with veiled hair, passing at length no one but shut doors, carved door-posts, and a solitary policeman.'

Jacob, with Florinda on his arm, reached his room and, lighting his lamp, said nothing at all. 'I don't like you when you look like that,' said Florinda. Jacob, who had been engaged earlier in the day on an essay defending literary indecency, now doubted whether he liked indecency in the raw, and experienced 'a violent reversion towards male society, cloistered rooms, and the works of the classics; and was ready to turn with wrath upon whoever it was who had fashioned life thus. Then Florinda laid her hand upon his knee.' And he knew that cloisters and classics were no use whatever. The problem, remarks Virginia Woolf, is insoluble.

Hyde Park at the height of the season is very different from Soho on a raw November night. Sun blisters the paint on the backs of the green chairs in the park, 'circled incessantly by turning wheels'. The motor cars pass endlessly over the bridge of the Serpentine. And the people: 'the upper classes walked upright, or bent themselves gracefully over the palings; the lower classes lay with their knees cocked up, flat on their backs; the sheep grazed on pointed wooden legs; small children ran down the sloping grass, stretched their arms, and fell. "Very urbane," said Jacob.' Florinda might have liked the look on his face then. At sunset on another day in Hyde Park Jacob, who has been sitting there, rises, tears up his seat ticket and walks off, at the same moment that his mother in Scarborough is writing a letter to another son and commenting on the beautiful sunset. 'The long windows of Kensington Palace flushed fiery rose as Jacob walked away; a flock of wild duck flew over the Serpentine; and the trees were stood against the sky, blackly, magnificently.'

Jacob does not spend all of his London days and nights sitting in Hyde Park, entertaining prostitutes, watching the crowds, going to the opera and dining out; he also reads Marlowe in the British Museum, when he is not gazing around him at other readers under the great dome—the atheist, Fraser, the feminist, Julia Hedge, Miss Marchmont, half out of her wits with a theory that colour is sound. The shiftings, murmurings, apologetic sneezes, and unashamed devastating coughs go on till closing time. While waiting for

45

his umbrella in the cloak-room, Jacob thinks of the British Museum as an enormous mind, hoarded beyond the power of any single mind to possess. He goes out into Great Russell Street, glazed and shining in the rain, reaches his rooms nearby, and reads Plato late into the night. And while he reads, Virginia Woolf's mind returns to the British Museum. 'The vast mind was sheeted with stone; and each compartment in the depths of it was safe and dry. The night watchmen, flashing their lanterns over the backs of Plato and Shakespeare, saw that on the twenty-second of February neither flame, rat, nor burglar was going to violate these treasures—poor, highly respectable men, with wives and families at Kentish Town, do their best for twenty years to protect Plato and Shakespeare, and then are buried at Highgate. Stone lies solid over the British Museum, as bone lies cool over the visions and heat of the brain. Only here the brain is Plato's brain and Shakespeare's; the brain has made pots and statues, great bulls, and little jewels, and crossed the river of death this way and that incessantly, seeking some landing, now wrapping the body well for its long sleep; now laying a penny piece on the eyes; now turning the toes scrupulously to the East. Meanwhile Plato continues his dialogue; in spite of the rain; in spite of the cab whistles; in spite of the woman in the mews behind Great Ormond Street, who has come home drunk and cries all night long, "Let me in!" ' And while Jacob reads on in the Phaedrus, old Jones's lantern as he makes his rounds sometimes lights up Ulysses, or a horse's head, or sometimes a flash of gold, or 'a mummy's sunken yellow cheek'. Finally the dialogue draws to a close, Plato's argument is stowed away in Jacob's mind, and 'for five minutes Jacob's mind continued alone, onwards, into the darkness. Then, getting up, he parted the curtains, and saw, with astonishing clearness, how the Springetts opposite had gone to bed; how it rained; how the Jews and the foreign woman, at the end of the street, stood by the pillar-box, arguing.'

Here is one of those fusions of inner and outer, that give us 'the moment whole.'

Other ladies besides Florinda, upper and lower class, married and single, are attracted to Jacob. Fanny, an artist's model, is in love with him, and like Mary in *Night and Day*, sometimes visits the British Museum, and 'keeping her eyes downcast until she was alongside the battered Ulysses, she opened them and got a fresh shock of Jacob's presence, enough to last her half a day'. She knows her love is hopeless. Walking along the Strand, looking in at the window of Bacon, the map-seller, she reflects that one's godmothers ought to have told one that it is no use making a fuss, that this is life, and Fanny said it now, 'looking at the large yellow globe marked with steamship lines'. To a customer inside, looking out, Fanny's face looked hard—girls are so old nowadays. To Fanny's eyes the equator swam with tears. She boards an omnibus, and we take leave of Fanny for ever. The omnibus stopped outside Charing Cross and behind it piled up buses, vans and motor cars, because a procession with banners was passing down Whitehall. 'Elderly people were stiffly descending from between the paws of the slippery lions, where they had been testifying to their faith, singing lustily . . . the traffic was released; lurched on; spun to a smooth continuous uproar; swerving round the curve of Cockspur Street; and sweeping past Government offices and equestrian statues down Whitehall to the prickly spires, the tethered grey fleet of masonry, the large white clock of Westminster. Five strokes Big Ben intoned; Nelson received the salute. The wires of the Admiralty quivered with some far-away communication.'

What was written on the banners that glittered down White-hall, what communication came over the wires, we can only guess; but we know that war is coming nearer and Jacob will be lost.

IV

Mrs Dalloway

Clarissa Dalloway, who gives her name to the best-known of Mrs Woolf's novels, is less interesting as a person than the Mrs Ramsay of *To the Lighthouse*, or the unfinished Rachel, or the perhaps too-finished Katharine Hilbery. She is not the favourite of her creator, who applies the adjective 'tinselly' to her. But she is a sharply clear figure, emerging most successfully from the combined stream-of-consciousness and stream-of-events pattern of the novel. Clarissa is a lady of the fashionable world of the government set, her husband a member of Parliament, her home in Westminster. She is fifty years old, a little tired and faded; her only child, Elizabeth, is almost grown; there is a rejected lover who reappears, Peter Walsh, long absent on service in India. The important event in the story, anticipated through a long June day and triumphantly achieved at night, is a party, one of Mrs Dalloway's famous parties. There are flash-backs down the corridors of the past to the time when Mrs Dalloway and some of her guests were young. We are in London all the day and the evening; in Westminster at the Dalloway home, in the Green Park, in Bond Street and other Mayfair streets, in Regent's Park, Russell Square and one of its big hotels, in the lodgings of Septimus Smith and the office of the Harley Street specialist, to whom Septimus is taken by his worried young Italian wife. Septimus, an ex-soldier suffering from shell-shock, sees the same aeroplane that Clarissa sees circling over

Westminster, hears the same strokes of Big Ben; sits on a bench in Regent's Park near Peter Walsh; and not long before Mrs Dalloway's party, throws himself out of the window of his lodgings and so escapes from the distinguished psychiatrist who would have placed him in an institution, and who mentions this sad case of suicide at Clarissa's party, thus introducing death into her brilliant drawing-room. Septimus surprisingly becomes, for a brief moment of illumination, her other self, her night side.

'I love walking in London,' said Mrs Dalloway, as she set forth to buy flowers for the party. Big Ben strikes: 'The leaden circles dissolved in the air. Such fools we are, she thought, crossing Victoria Street. For Heaven only knows why one loves it so, how one sees it so, making it up, building it round one, tumbling it, creating it every moment afresh; but the veriest frumps, the most dejected of miseries sitting on doorsteps (drink their downfall) do the same; can't be dealt with, she felt positive, by Acts of Parliament for that very reason: they love life. In people's eyes, in the swing, tramp, and trudge; in the bellow and the uproar; the carriages, motorcars, omnibuses, vans, sandwich men shuffling and swinging; brass bands; barrel organs; in the triumph and jingle and the strange high singing of some aeroplane overhead was what she loved; life; London; this moment of June.'

London in June includes Mrs Dalloway's flower-buying in Bond Street; Mr Dalloway's walk from Brook Street, where he lunched with Lady Bruton and Hugh Whitbread, back through the Green Park to Westminster; Elizabeth's shopping expedition to the Army and Navy Stores with her governess and her truant omnibus ride clear to St Paul's all by herself; Peter Walsh's long stroll through Whitehall, up the Haymarket and Regent Street and on to Regent's Park, where he rests on a bench and notices the odd behaviour of Septimus Smith; and his long evening walk from his Russell

49 D

Square hotel to Clarissa's party. Without much effort one could mark off the intervals by the strokes of Big Ben and find out precisely who was doing what at the very moment that some one else was doing something. The flow of the reverie of this or that character and the flow of life along the streets are so deftly mingled that one cannot, without doing violence to the effect, break them up by quotation. Yet to suggest Mrs Woolf's growth in technical virtuosity, two or three passages must be singled out.

The theme, for instance, of the continuity of London history reaching far into the past is woven into the present moment, when the old woman street singer sings a ballad near Regent's Park: 'a frail quivering sound, a voice bubbling up without direction, vigour, beginning or end . . . the voice of no age or sex, the voice of an ancient spring spouting from the earth . . . Through all ages—when the pavement was grass, when it was swamp, through the age of tusk and mammoth, through the age of silent sunrise, the battered woman . . . stood singing of love—love which has lasted a million years, she sang.' This ancient song, issuing from so rude a mouth, soaked 'through the knotted roots of infinite ages, and skeletons and treasure, streamed away in rivulets over the pavement and all along Marylebone Road, and down towards Euston, fertilising, leaving a damp stain'. Peter Walsh gave the poor creature a coin as he stepped into his taxi. 'Poor old woman,' said Rezia Smith, waiting to cross.

This June day is favourable to love. Peter returning after thirty years knows that he still loves Clarissa; and Richard, her husband, realizes not only that he loves Clarissa, but that he should tell her so; he has been thinking of her in starts all through the luncheon with Lady Bruton. He wishes to go straight to her in Westminster—holding something. Flowers? So he buys a huge armful of roses, crossed Piccadilly, and pursues his reverie through the Green Park—a reverie all mixed up with Clarissa, his life, and his public concerns as a member of Parliament, and turned this way and that by what he sees. 'Grey, dogged, dapper, clean,' he walks across the Park to tell his wife that he loves her. He enjoys the sight of the poor families sprawling and picnicking under the trees with paper bags thrown about; every park and square should be open in the summer to the poor mothers of Westminster and their crawling babies. 'But what could be done for female vagrants like that poor creature, stretched on her elbow (as if she had flung herself on the earth, rid of all ties, to observe curiously, to speculate boldly, to consider the whys and the wherefores, impudent, loose-lipped, humorous), he did not know. Bearing his flowers like a weapon, Richard Dalloway approached her; intent he passed her; still there was time for a spark between them—she laughed at the sight of him, he smiled good-humouredly, considering the problem of the female vagrant; not that they would ever speak . . . As for Buckingham Palace (like an old prima donna facing the audience all in white) you can't deny it a certain dignity, he considered, nor despise what does, after all, stand to millions of people (a little crowd was waiting at the gate to see the King drive out) for a symbol, absurd though it is; a child with a box of bricks could have done better, he thought; looking at the memorial to Queen Victoria (whom he could remember in her horn spectacles driving through Kensington), its white mound, its billowing motherliness . . . '

Recall Virginia Woolf's affection for the outdoor statues of London, and observe Peter Walsh, walking up Whitehall, over-taken by a procession of boys in uniform about to place a wreath on the Cenotaph. One had to respect it, this business of monuments and wreaths and discipline, though one might laugh. 'There they go, thought Peter Walsh, pausing at the edge of the pavement; and all the exalted statues, Nelson, Gordon, Havelock, the black, the spectacular images of great soldiers stood looking ahead of them, as if they too had made the same renunciation (Peter Walsh felt he too had made it, the great renunciation), trampled under the same temptations, and achieved at length a marble stare.' As Peter walks on he falls into an adventurous mood and follows an attractive lady across Piccadilly, up Regent Street, across Oxford Street, playing with the idea of a little escapade. But she turns a corner, and he goes on to Regent's Park. By the time we have settled Peter on a bench for a rest, we have made a West End tour, and by following the drift of his thoughts and observations, have learned most of the important things about him. He smokes a cigar, falls asleep and snores, and dreams, one gathers from the odd and fascinating pages that come next, about a solitary traveller.

Septimus is there, too, in Regent's Park, near Peter, but though he sees what goes on around him, he is drawing ever further away from the state recommended by his doctor—'to take an interest in things outside himself'. What he sees becomes distorted in his mind; that aeroplane, for instance, spelling out over London letters advertising some product, is signalling to him a secret message. He is beyond the help of London crowds, of the healing flow of the general life; as we know not only from looking into his mind, but from the way people stare at him and his worried wife, who is waiting for the moment to keep the appointment with Sir William Bradshaw in Harley Street. Peter Walsh thought the poor girl looked absolutely desperate.

In the evening Peter sets out from his hotel in Russell Square for Clarissa's party, walking towards Westminster. His expectant mood is in tune with that of London. 'Was everybody dining out, then? Doors were being opened here by a footman to let issue a high-stepping old dame, in buckled shoes, with three purple ostrich feathers in her hair. Doors were being opened for ladies wrapped like mummies in shawls

with bright flowers on them, ladies with bare heads . . .
Everybody was going out. What with these doors being
opened, and the descent and the start, it seemed as if the
whole of London were embarking in little boats moored to the
bank, tossing on the waters, as if the whole place were floating
off in carnival.' It is so warm that people stand about talking,
and couples loiter in the large square around which the cabs
swerved. He passes 'here a shindy of brawling women,
drunken women; here only a policeman and looming houses,
high houses, domed houses, parliaments'. From the river
comes the hoot of a steamer, a hollow misty cry. At last it is
her street, Clarissa's. Peter had grown young, become adventurous, recalled the past, thought of his career, of life and
death (he hears the bell of the ambulance carrying away the
body of poor Septimus, free at last from his terrors), and made
decisions—all during his walks, morning, afternoon and
evening, around London. The city, its sights and its crowds,
has played its part in the intricate interweaving of past and
present, the individual and the general life, the transitory
and the permanent.

Since Clarissa's world is the world of fashion, we have stayed
in the West End, and had no glimpse of Charing Cross, much
less of the City. But Elizabeth Dalloway, absorbed to her
mother's distress in her friendship with Miss Kilman who is
tutoring her in history—she prays with her behind closed
doors and talks with her of Causes—goes out that afternoon
to the Army and Navy Stores where Miss Kilman wishes to
buy petticoats and other uninteresting things, and where they
have a rather dreary tea. Elizabeth leaves her at the table,
pays the bill at the desk, and is gone—youth and beauty gone;
and Miss Kilman, awkward, ugly, and unhappy, goes out and
enters the Abbey to pray. Elizabeth, having a little time to
spare and enjoying being out of doors alone, waits in Victoria
Street for an omnibus—any omnibus—suddenly boards one,

takes a seat on top, and is off; the omnibus, insolently, all sails spread, rushes up Whitehall. Another penny to the Strand? Another penny then. Elizabeth begins to think what she might be: a doctor? a farmer? she loves animals. Somerset House looks splendid and serious. She liked to think of people working. 'She liked those churches, like shapes of grey paper, breasting the stream of the Strand. It was quite different here from Westminster, she thought, getting off at Chancery Lane. It was so serious; it was so busy. She would become a doctor, a farmer, possibly go into Parliament, if she found it necessary, all because of the Strand. The feet of those people busy about their activities, hands putting stone to stone, minds eternally occupied not with trivial chatterings (comparing women to poplars—which was rather exciting, of course, but very silly), but with thoughts of ships, of business, of law, of administration, and with it all so stately (she was in the Temple), gay (there was the river), pious (there was the Church), made her quite determined, whatever her mother might say, to become either a farmer or a doctor . . . And it was much better to say nothing about it.' This was the sort of thing that sometimes happened when one was alone, and the stimulation of the crowds did more than any of Miss Kilman's books to stir what lay 'slumbrous, clumsy, and sly on the mind's sandy floor'; an impulse, a revelation, which has its effects for ever, just breaks the surface, and then down again to the sandy floor.

Elizabeth walked a little way towards St Paul's, but did not dare to 'wander off into queer alleys, tempting bye-streets, any more than in a strange house open doors which might be bedroom doors, or sitting-room doors, or lead straight to the larder. For no Dalloways came down the Strand daily; she was a pioneer, a stray, venturing, trusting.' But there was in the Dalloway family the tradition of public service. Penetrating a little further in the direction of St Paul's, she runs into a procession of the unemployed, and likes the noise, the geniality, the trumpets, the people marching. There is something consolatory, something indifferent to the individual fate, in this voice of London, which—'pouring endlessly, year in and year out', taking whatever it might be, this vow, this van, this life, this procession, would 'wrap them all about and carry them on, as in the rough stream of a glacier the ice holds a splinter of bone, a blue petal, some oak trees, and rolls them on'. London has worked a subtle change in Elizabeth; she has had a kind of epiphany. Calmly and competently she mounted the Westminster omnibus. Seeing her at her mother's party that night, very handsome, very self-possessed, Peter reflects that she is not a bit like Clarissa. One is confident that she is not going to be like her.

In *Mrs Dalloway* we have lived (to borrow a phrase Mrs Woolf uses of another novelist) along a thread of observation which is always going in and out of this mind and of that mind. The result of the expert use of this method is something perfect of its kind. Mrs Woolf never uses it exclusively again; it remains one of her tools. In her next novel she left London for that northern island stroked by the beams of the lighthouse, and when her imagination turned back to London, it was to create the fantasy of *Orlando*. Here, and in the companion piece, the essay *A Room of One's Own*, there is less exploration of personal relationships, and much more speculation about time, sex, the position of women, the androgynous artist, literature, and, as always, life.

V

Orlando

and

A Room of One's Own

Orlando, according to the title, is a biography, but a very unconventional one: a composite biography of a poet who, like any poet, is both himself and the long tradition he inherits. Orlando's extraordinary career as man-woman, extending over three hundred years from the days of Elizabeth I to October, 1928, is fastened down, so far as fantasy can be tethered, to three places,: the great country house in Kent, Constantinople, and London. The connection of Orlando's country house with Knole and its distinguished family is well-known. Constantinople, where Orlando goes as ambassador in the 17th century, is conveniently remote for the sex-transformation scene; London would have been too familiar for such a performance. As for London, is it just background for English literature? Is it a symbol? Is it history? Is it fairy-land? Probably the last, one thinks, amazed at the scenes on the frozen Thames during the Great Frost. (But visit the London Museum, and you will find little models of such scenes). One is willing to accept the fact that there was a famous frost in the early days of James I's reign; to accept as probably based on contemporary records the most fantastic details—of people frozen beneath the surface and visible to sightseers, of the old bumboat woman, in her plaid and farthingales, her lap full of apples, sitting on a wrecked wherry boat, in a deep freeze.

Virginia Woolf loved the Elizabethan prose writers, 'first and most wildly, stirred by Hakluyt, which father lugged home for me—I think of it with some sentiment—father tramping over the Library with his little girl sitting at Hyde Park Gate in mind. He must have been 65; I 15 or 16 then.' The even more fantastic vision of the breaking-up of the ice during the the great Thaw, with all the strange cargoes of people and things carried out to sea in the rush of waters, while Orlando, riding his horse along the banks of the Thames, strains his eyes to see the ship of the Muscovite Embassy standing out to sea, with his white fox of a Russian princess, faithless, abroad,— even that one will accept, either as fairy-tale, or magnificent metaphor of Elizabethan literature, strange, beautiful, mad, incredible.

London enjoyed a carnival, we are told, during the Great Frost, and King James held his court at Greenwich. He had a park and pleasure ground erected on the ice and a Royal Pagoda, and there were fireworks, and vast bonfires of salted wood, with flames of green, orange and purple fire; and the most brilliant society of England—statesmen and admirals and courtly lovers, the Queen and her ladies—gathered under the crimson awnings. Whether or not *Othello* was ever played in a booth or on a stage near the Royal enclosure on the ice at Greenwich (it was performed for the first time in 1604), Orlando and his princess and a fine crowd of groundlings witnessed such a performance in this fairy-land. They were 'shouldered by apprentices, tailors; horse dealers, cony catchers; starving scholars; maid-servants in their whimples; orange girls; ostlers; sober citizens; bawdy tapsters; and a crowd of little ragamuffins such as always haunt the outskirts of a crowd . . . all the riff-raff of the London streets . . . jesting and jostling, here casting dice, telling fortunes, shoving, tickling, pinching; here uproarious, there glum; some of them with mouths gaping a yard wide; others as little reverent as daws on a house-top; all as variously rigged out as their purse or stations allowed; here in fur and broadcloth; there in tatters with their feet kept from the ice only by a dishclout bound about them.'

There is little more of early 17th century London at this point. But a couple of centuries later, Orlando looking out over the city remembers how it was in the days of Queen Elizabeth, a huddle of houses under her windows at Black-friars: 'The stars reflected themselves in deep pits of stagnant water which lay in the middle of the streets. A black shadow at the corner where the wine shop used to stand, was, as likely as not, the corpse of a murdered man. She could remember the cries of many a one wounded in such night brawlings, when she was a little boy, held to the diamond-paned window in her nurse's arms. Troops of ruffians, men and women, unspeakably interlaced, lurched down the streets, trolling out wild songs with jewels flashing in their ears, and knives gleaming in their fists. On such a night as this the impermeable tangle of the forests on Highgate and Hamp-stead would be outlined, writhing in contorted intricacy against the sky. Here and there, on one of the hills which rose above London, was a stark gallows tree, with a corpse nailed to rot or parch on its cross; for danger and insecurity, lust and violence, poetry and filth swarmed over the tortuous Eliza-bethan highways and buzzed and stank—Orlando could remember even now the smell of them on a hot night—in the little rooms and narrow pathways of the city.'

Orlando, disgraced at court for his escapade with the Russian princess, passes at Knole the Jacobean Age, with its melancholy and its inward turning, 'something intricate and many-chambered'; taking a strange delight in thoughts of death and decay, reading Sir Thomas Browne, and 'afflicted with a love of literature'. The disease of reading led to the disease of writing; and we leave him in his great house, where all his beautiful possessions seemed but as phantoms. Later in the century, emerging from this seclusion to take part in public affairs, he is sent as ambassador to Constantinople, where he has exciting adventures, changes his sex, and lives for a time with primitive gipsies in remote hills. This phase of Orlando's life suggests the stories of several brilliant and eccentric English ladies, who adventured into the East and furnished picturesque chapters in English biography.

He is a woman when he returns to London. As Rachel had steamed down the Thames in *The Voyage Out*, Orlando sails up the Thames on a fine September morning, and the captain points out to her the Tower, Greenwich Hospital, Westminster Abbey, the dome of St Paul's, which Mr Wren had built during her absence, and a pillar with a shock of golden hair bursting from the top—the Monument commemorating the plague and the Great Fire. Gone was all the splendour and corruption which she remembered. Here now were orderly thoroughfares and stately coaches standing at the doors of houses with polished knockers and bow windows. All this visible through the Captain's glass! As the ship sailed to its anchorage by London Bridge, she saw the coffeehouse windows 'where, on balconies, since the weather was fine, a great number of decent citizens sat at ease, with china dishes in front of them, clay pipes by their sides, while one among them read from a news sheet, and was frequently interrupted by the laughter or the comments of the others. Were these taverns, were these wits, were these poets? The Captain, noting that they were passing the Cocoa Tree, pointed out Mr Addison taking his coffee.'

Orlando goes into society, meets Mr Pope, becomes familiar with the wit and satire of the age, and with the opinions men have of women. After a party she takes Mr Pope home with her in her chariot. As they drive through the streets between May-fair and Blackfriars, the intervals of light from the oil lamps alternating with the stretches of darkness suggest the light thrown by genius on human affairs, and the weaknesses even of genius. Particularly the weakness genius often displays on the Woman question. Orlando shares Mrs Woolf's feminist attitudes. By the time they reach the lamp-post at the corner of what is now Piccadilly Circus, Orlando feels that both Mr Pope and she are wretched pigmies, naked, solitary and defenceless; and looking Mr Pope full in the face she thinks, 'It is equally vain for you to think you can protect me, or for me to think I can worship you. The light of truth beats upon us without shadow, and the light of truth is damnably un-becoming to us both.' All this while they go on talking agreeably, while the coach goes from light to darkness 'down the Haymarket, along the Strand, up Fleet Street,' finally reaching her house in Blackfriars.

The gossip Orlando hears when she is in the company of men of genius gives us that mixture of biography and criticism which is the charm of Mrs Woolf's literary essays. Orlando pours tea for the wits, listens to their views on women, and sometimes takes them down to her country house. Coming back to London after one of these intervals, rather tired of wit and feeling a desire to return to the freer ways of her male self, she dons some rather old-fashioned male attire, and goes out on a fine night in April. Turning into Leicester Square she approaches a young woman seated on a bench beneath a plane tree, looking dejected, but ready enough to return Orlando's greeting. She is preparing to entertain this supposed gentleman in her lodgings in Gerrard Street, when he suddenly, in a gust of anger, merriment and pity, proclaims himself a woman, to the immense relief of Nell. Around a bowl of punch she tells some lively stories, and though she possesses no wit, Orlando finds the society of Nell and her

friends refreshing after Pope and Addison and Chesterfield
—as refreshing as the racy memoirs of the underside of 18th
century life (some of them the work of women) are to us.
Orlando and the girls have a happy evening, despite the well-
known fact, recorded by Mr This and That, that women,
when they lack the stimulus of the other sex, can find nothing
to say to each other; 'when they are alone, they do not talk,
they scratch'. And here Mrs Woolf does a little scratching:
'Women are incapable of any feeling of affection for their own
sex, and hold each other in the greatest aversion . . . (Mr
T. R. has proved it).'

At this stage of her career Orlando changed her sex 'far
more frequently than those who have worn only one set of
clothing can conceive . . . the pleasures of life were in-
creased and its experiences multiplied'. On one of her night
junketings in male attire, she stood for half an hour beneath
the window of a house in Bolt Court, watching three shadows
on the blind drinking tea. It was more absorbing than a play.
'There was the little shadow with the pouting lips, fidgeting
this way and that on his chair, uneasy, petulant, officious;
there was the bent female shadow, crooking a finger in the cup
to feel how deep the tea was, for she was blind; and there was
the Roman-looking rolling shadow in the big arm-chair—he
who twisted his fingers so oddly and jerked his head from
side to side, and swallowed down the tea in such vast gulps.
Dr Johnson, Mr Boswell and Mrs Williams—those were the
shadows' names.' The great Roman shadow rose, rocking
somewhat, and rolled out 'the most magnificent phrases that
ever left human lips'. So Orlando thought, though she didn't
hear a word.

After one of these night rambles (towards the end of the
18th century?), Orlando stood at her bedroom window in
shirt and breeches, looking out over the town which lay under
a white haze this frosty midwinter night. Something was

stirring in the air that kept her from going to bed. 'She could see St Paul's, the Tower, Westminster Abbey, with all the spires and domes of the city churches, the smooth bulk of its banks, the opulent and ample curves of its halls and meeting-places. On the north rose the smooth, shorn heights of Hampstead, and in the west the streets and squares of Mayfair shone out in one clear radiance. Upon this serene and orderly prospect the stars looked down, glittering, positive, hard, from a cloudless sky. In the extreme clearness of the atmosphere the line of every roof, the cowl of every chimney was perceptible; even the cobbles in the streets showed distinct one from another . . . ' All was light, order, serenity.

But at the stroke of midnight, a light breeze rose, clouds began to gather and before long covered the city; 'all was darkness; all was doubt; all was confusion'. The 19th century had begun. A change now came over the English climate— suggested by metaphors unrelated to the London scene—a dampness, chill, luxuriant fertility. Presently we find Orlando driving through St James's Park in her old panelled coach. The sun struggling through the clouds lights up a most extraordinary pile of objects massed about where the statue of Queen Victoria now stands—all symbols of the age which had overtaken Orlando. The vision makes her blushingly conscious of her black breeches as she passes Buckingham Palace, and she flees post haste to her country house, wraps herself in a damask quilt, calls her housekeeper, and sits down to a dish of muffins. The spirit of the age has captured her. 'Orlando had inclined herself naturally to the Elizabethan spirit, to the Restoration spirit, to the spirit of the eighteenth century . . . But the spirit of the nineteenth century was antipathetic to her in the extreme, and thus it took her and broke her.' She begins to think of wedding rings and of someone to lean on. She wanders in her own park with timorous glances about her, lest some male form should be hiding behind a furze bush; she falls and injures her ankle, is rescued by a romantic horseman, and a few minutes later is engaged to him. Thus Orlando made obeisance to the spirit of the age: 'she had just managed . . . by putting on a ring and finding a man on a moor, by loving nature and being no satirist, cynic, or psychologist . . . to pass its examination successfuly'. She took to writing. Seated at her table—her husband meanwhile adventuring beyond the seas—she looked fitted for love; and surely since she was a woman and beautiful, she would soon give over 'the pretence of writing and thinking and begin at least to think of a gamekeeper (and as long as she thinks of a man, nobody objects to a woman thinking)'.

At last Orlando drops her pen and, musing about life, looks out of the window and discovers that the world is going on as usual. And since her manuscript must be read, and elk hounds and rose bushes cannot read, she catches the eleven-forty-five to London (the steam engine having come into being during her long absorption in the inner life), is whirled up to London, and alights on the platform at Charing Cross.

Her old house at Blackfriars was now sold, part to the Salvation Army and part to an umbrella factory. She walked out into the uproar of the Strand. 'Vehicles of all sizes, drawn by blood horses and by dray horses, conveying one solitary dowager or crowded to the top by whiskered men in silk hats, were inextricably mixed . . . Every inch of the pavement was crowded' . . . Men held out trays of toys, women sat besides baskets of spring flowers, all bawling their wares, newsboys shouted Disaster. Orlando walked up one street and down another, past shop windows, up and down avenues of sedate mansions, each the copy of the other, 'with two pillars and six steps and a pair of curtains neatly drawn and family luncheons laid on tables, and a parrot looking out of one window and a man servant out of another'. There were great open squares 'with black, shiny, tightly buttoned statues of fat men in the middle, and war horses prancing, and columns rising and fountains falling and pigeons fluttering'—all so bewildering that Orlando forgot her manuscript, 'The Oak Tree', until by accident she met a gentleman, neat, portly, prosperous, cane in hand and flower in buttonhole, whom she had known in Elizabethan times and again in the 18th century as Nick Greene, the critic; now Sir Nicholas and the most influential critic of the Victorian age. During lunch together Sir Nicholas bewails the fact that the great age of literature is over; we live in degenerate times and must cherish the past. Orlando could have sworn that she had heard him say the same thing three hundred years ago—the names were different, the spirit the same. Orlando's manuscript falls out from the bosom of her dress, and Sir Nicholas takes it to see if he can get it published, first briefing her on booksellers, royalties, reviewers and influence.

After visiting a bookshop, which astounds her by the number and variety of its wares, and ordering everything of importance sent to her house in Mayfair, Orlando turns into Hyde Park and flinging herself down under a tree near the Serpentine, tries to read the papers and critical journals she has carried from the bookshop. Life and literature become confusingly mingled, for dogs bark, carriage wheels sound, a rubber ball bounces on her newspaper, a pair of scarlet trousers walk by—'how would Addison have put that?'—and here two dogs are dancing on their hind legs—'how would Lamb have described that?' She stands on the bank of the Serpentine, which is the colour of bronze, with spider-thin boats skimming from side to side. 'For really, she thought, pushing a little boat with her toe . . . ' and taking off from the toy boat on the Serpentine, Orlando is launched upon an ecstatic reverie about her husband and his ship on the Atlantic, and finds herself talking aloud as she waits for the carriages to pass at the Stanhope Gate. (For the consequence of not living with one's husband is that 'one talks nonsense aloud in Park Lane'). 'A golden river had coagulated and massed itself in golden blocks across Park Lane.' A stately spectacle, the triumph of an age: 'portly and splendid there they sat. But now the policeman let fall his hand; the stream became liquid; the massive conglomeration of splendid objects moved, dispersed and disappeared into Piccadilly.' And Orlando walked on to her house in Curzon Street, where, from an earlier phase of her life, she could remember curlews calling and meadowsweet blowing.

During a significant interval when something very remarkable happens to Orlando, we hear some of that London street music from 'one of these frail, reedy, fluty, jerky, old-fashioned barrel-organs, which are still sometimes played by Italian organ-grinders in back streets'. The sound transports us in thought over the roof-tops and back gardens to Kew, where, flinging a cloak down under an oak, we (the anonymous participants in this curious affair) sit waiting for the king-fisher—a symbol if ever there was one—to cross from bank to bank. We see the factory chimneys and their smoke; the city clerks; an old lady taking her dog for a walk; a servant girl wearing her new hat; we speculate on the secrets in their hearts, and through our cigarette smoke see blaze up 'the splendid fulfilment of natural desires for a boat, for a rat in the ditch; as once one saw blazing—such silly hops and skips the mind takes when it slops like this all over the saucer and the barrel-organ plays—saw blazing a fire in a field against minarets near Constantinople'.

(So Orlando was safely delivered of a son).

On a much later day Orlando looks out of a window on a Park Lane much changed, with truncated carriages without horses gliding about of their own accord. King Edward had succeeded Queen Victoria. That remarkable climate had changed again, and the sky was no longer so thick, so watery. At night lights were everywhere. At a touch a whole room was lit; there were no more lingering shadows and odd corners and women in aprons carrying wobbly lamps; and the women had grown very narrow, and men's faces were as bare as the palms of one's hands; ivy had perished or been scraped off; vegetables were less fertile, and families smaller. But Orlando didn't linger in the Edwardian Age. Suddenly the long tunnel she seemed to have been travelling in for hundreds of years widened and light poured in; the clock ticked louder and louder until there was a terrific explosion in her ear—and it was ten o'clock on the eleventh of October, 1928. 'It was the present moment.'

Orlando at the present moment goes shopping at Marshall and Snelgrove's in Oxford Street. Ascending in the lift, she sees at each floor stop another slice of the world displayed with all the smells of that world clinging to it, and is reminded of the river off Wapping in the time of Elizabeth I, where the treasure ships and merchant ships used to anchor. How richly and curiously they had smelt! Leaving the lift at the top floor she tries to put her mind on her shopping list, and is fingering some Irish linen sheets when a whiff of scent recalls the faithless Russian princess. She has a vision of Sasha as a 'fat, furred woman, marvellously well-preserved, seductive, diademed, a Grand Duke's mistress'. Back on the ground floor, she looks through the glass doors at the traffic on Oxford Street. 'Omnibus seemed to pile itself up on omnibus and then to jerk itself apart. So the ice blocks had pitched and tossed that day on the Thames.' Time, thinks Orlando, has passed over me; 'nothing is any longer one thing . . . Someone lights a pink candle and I see a girl in Russian trousers. When I step out of doors—as I do now . . . what is it that I taste? Little herbs. I hear goat bells. I see mountains. Turkey?' Orlando had gone too far from the present moment for anyone preparing to drive a motor-car on Oxford Street. But she did collect herself and being an expert driver, she shot in her car, swung, squeezed and slid, down Regent Street, down Haymarket, down Northumberland Avenue, over Westminster Bridge, and into the old Kent Road. 'The process of motoring fast out of London so much resembles the chopping up small of identity which precedes unconsciousness and perhaps death itself that it is an open question in what sense Orlando can be said to have existed at the present moment.' In what sense did she ever exist? At all events, as she leaves London, we leave her with deep regret, to go to her country house and find her husband there.

October, 1928, 'present time' in *Orlando*, was the month in which Mrs Woolf gave the lectures at Newnham and Girton, Cambridge, on Woman and Fiction, which she altered and expanded into *A Room of One's Own*. The close relationship between the themes of sex and literature in *Orlando* and the argument in this essay needs no demonstrating. The attitude towards women which she found so irritating at 'Oxbridge' has roused all sorts of questions concerning the truth of what has been said through the ages about women—chiefly by men. So she goes to the British Museum to consult the learned and unprejudiced. It is a dreary day, and the streets near the Museum are dismal; full of open coal-holes and four-wheeled cabs discharging families with their corded boxes in front of the Bloomsbury boarding-houses. 'London was like a workshop. London was like a machine. We were all being shot backwards and forwards on this plain foundation to make some pattern. The British Museum was another department of the factory. The swing doors swung open; and there one stood under the vast dome, as if one were a thought in the huge bald forehead which is so splendidly encircled by a band of famous names.' The embittered suffragist in *Jacob's Room* had noted the absence among those names of any woman. (But one looks up at the dome today—July, 1958—and sees only the dim ghost of Browning showing through the gold of one of the rectangular plaques. The librarian couldn't tell us when the names were erased, but thought the safe course had been taken in removing them all; for they couldn't, he said, leave women out now; and apparently the point hasn't yet been reached when they could be put in).

The catalogue under WOMAN is consulted, the books and articles by men listed and read, with thought-provoking results. Later, whilst walking and meditating on what she has read, Mrs Woolf weaves London into her argument. 'Walk through the Admiralty Arch (I had reached that monument), or any other avenue given up to trophies and cannon, and reflect upon the kind of glory celebrated there.' The unpleasant instincts connected with the making of money and more money are bred of the conditions of life, 'of the lack of civilization, I thought, looking at the statue of the Duke of Cambridge, and in particular at the feathers in his cocked hat, with a fixity that they have scarcely ever received before.' Thus thinking and speculating, she makes her way back to her house by the river. 'Lamps were being lit and an indescribable change had come over London since the morning hour. It was as if the great machine after labouring all day had made with our help a few yards of something very exciting and beautiful —a fiery fabric flashing with red eyes, a tawny monster roaring with hot breath. Even the wind seemed flung like a flag as it lashed the houses and rattled the hoardings.' In her little street a nursemaid was wheeling the perambulator back for nursery tea; 'the coal-heaver was folding his empty sacks on top of each other; the woman who keeps the greengrocer's shop was adding up the day's takings with her hands in red mittens'. One wonders about the relative importance, past, present and future, of the various employments and women's share in them. The shop women may drive engines in the future, the nursemaid heave coal. Assumptions based on the facts observed when women were the protected sex will have disappeared. '(Here a squad of soldiers marched down the street).'

Later in the essay, discussing the range of possible material open to the woman novelist of today, Mrs Woolf thinks of the 'infinitely obscure lives' of the vast majority of women, which remain to be recorded; and there comes to her mind's eye 'one of those long streets somewhere south of the river, whose infinite rows are innumerably populated'. She makes up a story about an ancient lady crossing one of those streets on the arm of a middle-aged woman, perhaps her daughter, at dusk when the lamps are being lit, as they must have done year after year. What has life meant to her? Mrs Woolf goes on in thought 'through the streets of London feeling in imagination the pressure of dumbness, the accumulation of unrecorded life, whether from the women at the street corners with their arms akimbo, and the rings embedded in their fat swollen fingers, talking with a gesticulation like the swing of Shakespeare's words; or from the violet-sellers and match-sellers and old crones stationed under doorways; or from drifting girls whose faces, like waves in sun and cloud, signal the coming of men and women and the flickering lights of shop windows'.

A final look from the window of a room of one's own, in London, of course, on the 26th of October, 1928. London is 'winding itself up again; the factory was astir; the machines were beginning.' People pass by, an errand boy, a woman with a dog on a lead. 'The fascination of a London street is that no two people are ever alike . . . There were the business-like, with their little bags; there were the drifters rattling sticks upon area railings.' Then there was a lull; a single leaf fell from a plane tree at the end of the street, like a signal pointing to a force in things. 'It seemed to point to a river, which flowed past, invisibly, round the corner, down the street, and took people and eddied them along . . . Now it was bringing from one side of the street to the other diagonally a girl in patent leather boots, and then a young man in a maroon overcoat; it was also bringing a taxi-cab; and it brought all three together at a point directly beneath my window; where the taxi stopped; and the girl and the young man stopped; and they got into the taxi; and then the cab glided off as if it were swept on by the current elsewhere.' This familiar London street scene, this union of the girl and the man in 'the taxi of human personality' (Winifred Holtby's phrase), gives the watcher a curious satisfaction and leads her into speculation on the unity of the mind; on the androgynous character of a great mind as compared with a single-sexed mind; on the spiritual co-operation, the harmony, of the two-sexed mind; and so on to Coleridge and further thoughts on writers and on sex, and on the effects in literature of sex-consciousness.

VI

The Waves

Orlando gave us a London expanded in space and time, a
spacious city over which the imagination plays freely, and the
individual life is part not only of the many other lives around
us, but of the generations we have left behind. *The Waves*
deals in another sort of magic, that of the sea, not of the
streets. Separating the sections of the book are interludes:
the sea at dawn, early morning, daylight, high noon, afternoon, sunset, evening, night—images of human growth and
decline and death. Yet the street magic is not entirely absent,
for London is part of the lives of the six characters, whose
formal monologues record what they see and think and feel
through their very diverse temperaments.

What is it like to come into London for the first time, when
one is young? Bernard, beginning his career and about to be
married, is excited at the thought of becoming part of the
speed of the city; the train he is on is hurled at it as a sort of
missile: 'How fair, how strange,' said Bernard, 'glittering,
many-pointed and many-domed London lies before me under
mist. Guarded by gasometers, by factory chimneys, she lies
sleeping as we approach. She folds the ant-heap to her breast.
All cries, all clamour, are softly enveloped in silence . . .
Ridges fledged with houses rise from the mist. Factories,
cathedrals, glass domes, institutions and theatres erect themselves.' As he steps out on the platform at Euston, he feels
his individual self about to be submerged. Though he has

been keenly aware of himself—a young man in love—he now wishes to unclasp his hands, let fall his possessions, and 'merely stand here in the street, taking no part, watching the omnibuses, without desire; without envy; with what would be boundless curiosity about human destiny, if there were any longer an edge to my mind . . . I will let myself be carried on by the general impulse. The surface of my mind slips along like a pale-grey stream reflecting what passes . . . The roar of the traffic, the passage of undifferentiated faces, this way and that way, drugs me into dreams; rubs the features from faces. People might walk through me . . . The growl of traffic might be any uproar—forest trees or the roar of wild beasts . . . Beneath these pavements are shells, bones and silence.' Thus 'unmoored from a private being', he feels vibrations of sympathy with the crowds, 'the starers and trippers; these errand boys and furtive and fugitive girls who, ignoring their doom, look in at shop-windows'. Being a natural coiner of words, like his creator, he begins to make up stories.

Louis, just out of college, also draws near London. 'The train slows and lengthens, as we approach London, the centre, and my heart draws out too, in fear, in exultation. I am about to meet—what? What extraordinary adventure waits me, among these mail vans, these porters, these swarms of people calling taxis? I feel insignificant, lost, but exultant. With a soft shock we stop. I will let the others get out before me. I will sit still one moment before I emerge into that chaos, that tumult. I will not anticipate what is to come. The huge uproar is in my ears. It sounds and resounds under this glass roof like the surge of a sea. We are cast down on the platform with our handbags. We are whirled asunder. My sense of self almost perishes; my contempt. I become drawn in, tossed down, thrown sky-high. I step out on to the platform, grasping all that I possess—one bag.'

Louis has come to London to be a banker or business

organizer; his father, a banker at Brisbane, had failed, and
Louis feels inferior about that and about his own Australian
accent. His reverie-recitative in an eating-shop in the City,
where he is having lunch, is partly directed and partly dis-
ordered by these private ambitions and obsessions, and by
what he sees of the street through the window, and around
him in the restaurant. 'People go on passing . . . Motor-
cars, vans, motor-omnibuses; and again motor-omnibuses,
vans, motor-cars—they pass the window. In the background
I perceive shops and houses; also the grey spires of a city
church. In the foreground are glass shelves set with plates of
buns and ham sandwiches. All is somewhat obscured by steam
from a tea-urn. A meaty, vapourish smell of beef and mutton,
sausages and mash, hangs down like a damp net in the middle
of the eating-house. I prop my book against a bottle of
Worcester sauce and try to look like the rest.' Louis, unlike
Bernard, cannot forget himself, as the people go on passing
against the spires of the churches and the plates of ham sandwiches. He is conscious of flux, disorder, annihilation and
despair, and at the same time of the rhythm of the eating-
house, a sort of waltz tune, with the waitresses balancing
trays, swinging in and out, 'dealing plates of greens, of
apricot and custard, dealing them at the right time, to the
right customers'. There is a central rhythm, but he is not
included. His desire is to reduce everything to order, to
include all: 'I will not submit to this aimless passing of
billycock hats and Homburg hats and all the plumed and
variegated head-dresses of women . . . And the grinding
and the steam that runs in unequal drops down the window
pane; and the stopping and the starting with a jerk of motor-
omnibuses; and the hesitations at counters; and the words
that trail drearily without human meaning; I will reduce you
to order.' As recurrent images in his reveries convey—('I have
seen women carrying red pitchers to the banks of the Nile')—

Virginia Woolf's London

Louis is of those who through the ages have been seekers and builders of civilization.

In the restaurant where the six meet for a farewell dinner to their hero, Percival, who is sailing for India, Louis is aware of the roar of London all around them; Bernard, of the light of the city. To Louis all the separate sounds—'wheels, bells, the cries of drunkards, of merrymakers, are churned into one sound, steel blue, circular.' Bernard calls Percival's attention, while they wait for the taxi, to the street, 'hard and burnished with the churning of innumerable wheels. The yellow canopy of our tremendous energy hangs like a burning cloth above our heads. Theatres, music halls and lamps in private houses make that light.'

Remember the glimpse of the Tube in *Jacob's Room*. Now we go underground with Jinny, who has always responded to life with gaiety and eagerness. 'Here I stand . . . in the Tube station where everything that is desirable meets —Piccadilly South Side, Piccadilly North Side, Regent Street and the Haymarket. I stand for a moment under the pavement in the heart of London. Innumerable wheels rush and feet press just over my head. The great avenues of civilization meet here and strike this way and that. I am in the heart of life.' And then she catches sight of herself in a mirror—no longer young, no longer part of the procession. The millions descending the stairs, urged downwards in a terrible descent, are the millions of those who have died, among them Percival. For a moment she is overwhelmed by fear, by solitude, by the sense that there is no one who will come if she signals. She shudders at 'the soundless flight of upright bodies down the moving stairs,' like some army of the dead. For an instant only she is in the grip of this vision. Then she makes up her face in front of the mirror, thinks of the superb red and yellow omnibuses overhead, of the powerful beautiful cars, of the men and women, 'equipped, prepared, driving onward',

74

a triumphant procession. The broad thoroughfares above are 'sanded paths of victory driven through the jungle'. Even underground there is the radiance of beautiful gauzes and silks in the glass windows; 'lifts rise and fall, trains stop, trains start as regularly as the waves of the sea . . . I am a native of this world, I follow its banners'. So she will rise to the surface, stand erect with the others in Piccadilly Circus, signal to a cab, drive back to her own house, fill the vases with flowers, and wait for someone to ring the bell.

On Shaftesbury Avenue the scholarly Neville, standing at a book stall, reads Shakespeare. Or he takes a walk with Percival through the Park to the Embankment, along the Strand to St Paul's, always talking, sometimes pausing to look. 'But can this last? I said to myself, by a lion in Trafalgar Square, by the lion seen once and forever.' Rhoda, grieving over Percival's death, buys a penny bunch of violets in Oxford Street and makes a pilgrimage in trams and omnibuses to Greenwich, sees the masts among the chimneys, walks by the river, and, as her offering to Percival, throws the violets into the water.

Bernard (like a more responsive Jacob) lingers one day in St Paul's, 'the brooding hen with spread wings from whose shelter run omnibuses and streams of men and women at the rush hour'. 'My wandering and inquisitive eye then shows me an awe-stricken child; a shuffling pensioner; or the obeisances of tired shop-girls burdened with heaven knows what strife in their poor thin breasts, come to solace themselves in the rush hour. I stray and look and wonder, and sometimes, rather furtively, try to rise on the shaft of somebody else's prayer into the dome, out, beyond, wherever they go. But then like the lost and wailing dove, I find myself failing, fluttering, descending and perching upon some curious gargoyle, some battered nose or absurd tombstone, with humour, with wonder, and so again watch the sightseers

with their Baedeckers shuffling past, while the boy's voice
soars in the dome and the organ now and then indulges in a
moment of elephantine triumph.'

The six friends of the dead Percival have a reunion at
Hampton Court. They are middle-aged. The restaurant, the
fading sunset, the gathering darkness, the great trees in whose
shadows lovers linger, the unlighted avenues stretching
away into the distance, the ghosts from the past—King
William mounting his horse, the court ladies sweeping the
turf with their embroidered panniers—the flare hanging over
London, the hoot of a steamer from the river—all furnish
rather faint clues to where they are and what each is ex-
periencing. It is all steeped in the magical atmosphere of
subconscious thought. Only at the end do we touch earth when
Susan (firmly rooted in her country life and her family), and
Bernard (who always looks out on what is about him and seeks
words to express it), pace the terrace together. 'Now how
comforting it is to watch the lights coming out in the bed-
rooms of small shopkeepers on the other side of the river . . .
What do you think their takings have been today? Only just
enough to pay for the rent, for light and food and the children's
clothing. But just enough . . . ' Bernard fills in the picture
of little gardens, a rabbit in its hutch destined for the Sunday
dinner, and so on. It all gives him the feeling that life is
tolerable.

Bernard is the survivor, the commentator, who sums up the
lives of his friends and wonders about the globe we try to
shape, turning it about in our fingers, the globe of life, with
its walls of the thinnest air. Leaving the almost deserted
restaurant where he has dined and mused, he sees before him
the familiar street, a kindling in the sky of lamplight or of
dawn, hears a stir of sparrows chirping in the plane trees.
'What is dawn in the city to an elderly man standing in the
street, looking up rather dizzily at the sky . . . Dawn is

some sort of renewal.' The final image is not of dawn in the city, but of the wave rising, the wave of desire, of defiance of death.

VII

Flush's London

In the mood of exhilaration over writing the last sentence of *The Waves*, Virginia Woolf walked down Southampton Row, thinking to herself, 'And I have given you a new book.' (*Diary*, April 29, 1930). An odd gift, this, to the busy Bloomsbury thoroughfare, with its many little shops, offices, banks, restaurants and hotels, where one can satisfy all the everyday needs of life, from watches and typewriters, newspapers and sandwiches and shoes, to rented novels at Boot's the chemist's and tickets for Seeing London tours and the latest plays. Yet a street favourable somehow to the creative impulse of the street haunter. For a couple of years later Mrs Woolf records in her *Diary* the birth of a new idea, an essay-novel that was to take in everything, sex, education, life, 'and come, with the most agile and powerful leaps, like a chamois, across precipices from 1880 to here and now. That's the notion, anyhow, and I have been in such a haze and dream and intoxication, declaiming phrases, seeing scenes, as I walk up Southampton Row, that I can hardly say I have been alive at all since the 10th October.' Down Southampton Row—*The Waves* finished; and up Southampton Row—*The Years* begun.

Getting in the way of the new book was Mrs Browning's spaniel Flush, whose story Mrs Woolf had begun while revising *The Waves*, but who was gradually shoved out of the nest, as by a cuckoo born there. He kept lingering on; she couldn't despatch him; he became a frightful bore—'that abominable dog Flush.' But at last she was through with him, and free to write *The Years*. We, however, are grateful for Flush, both because of the light he throws on the courtship of Miss Barrett and Mr Browning and because of his very special dog's view of London and Florence. His is certainly a novel angle of vision, often needing a little interpretation by Mrs Woolf, who doesn't venture far into his stream of consciousness.

We first meet Flush in that shut-in invalid's room in Wimpole Street, and see and smell the room as he did, and listen to the noise of London in the foggy winter. 'The traffic droned on perpetually outside with muffled reverberations; now and again a voice went calling hoarsely, "old chairs and baskets to mend", down the street; sometimes there was a jangle of organ music, coming nearer and louder; going further and fading away.' When Flush went out into Wimpole Street, he was walked by a servant. That was in 1842, but 'even now perhaps nobody rings the bell of a house in Wimpole Street without trepidation. It is the must august of London streets, the most impersonal. Indeed, when the world seems tumbling to ruin, and civilization rocks on its foundations, one has only to go to Wimpole Street; to pace that avenue; to survey those houses; to consider their uniformity; to marvel at the window curtains and their consistency; to admire the brass knockers and their regularity; to observe butchers tendering joints and cooks receiving them; to reckon the incomes of the inhabitants and infer their consequent submission to the laws of God and man . . . The butchers of Wimpole Street move ponderously even today; in the summer of 1842, they were more deliberate still.'

When his mistress went shopping, drawn in her bath chair up Wimpole Street, Flush trotting after had his nostrils assaulted by 'the whole battery of a London street on a hot summer's day'. He smelt 'the swooning smells that lie in the gutters; the bitter smells that corrode iron railings; the fuming, heady smells that rise from basements . . . smells that lay far beyond the range of the human nose.' The passage of human bodies dazed him, a wheel whizzed an inch from his nose, trousers brushed his flanks—until, with every nerve throbbing and every sense singing, he reached Regent's Park, and (one may say) joined Septimus and Rezia and Peter Walsh and other frequenters of that park from Virginia Woolf's world. He had passed his puppyhood in the country with Miss Mitford. But though there were flowers and grass in the park, he was not free to run around; 'without being able to decipher a word of the placard at the Gate, he had learnt his lesson—in Regent's Park dogs must be led on chains'. He came to know a lot about the dogs of London and their class differences, and to recognise his own aristocratic status, and to be assured on the evidence of his points that he was the equal of the best-bred cocker in Wimpole Street.

We see Oxford Street from Flush's angle, too. But dangers lay in wait for aristocratic dogs in the West End, from the organized dog thieves who stole poodles and spaniels, if they happened to be loose for a moment in the crowded street, and blackmailed their wealthy owners. Behind Miss Barrett's bedroom was one of the worst slums in London; out of the slum came the dog thieves; it was in modern terms a very well-paying racket. From records contemporary with the year 1846 when Flush was stolen, Mrs Woolf selects dreadful details of the Whitechapel slums and the 'Rookeries' in St Giles's, at the bottom of Tottenham Court Road. Here, not a stone's throw from Wimpole Street, 'you might see sights and hear language and smell smells . . . that threw doubts upon the solidity even of Wimpole Street'. We endure with Flush the horrors of the den in the Rookeries where he was confined for days with other poor brutes, while negotiations for his ransom went on; and Miss Barrett, against all advice, ventured into the world she had never seen before, in Shoreditch. A Mr Taylor was the boss of the racket, and Miss Barrett tried to persuade her brother to go and see him at the appointed place and pay the sum demanded. All Wimpole Street was against her, having determined to make a principled stand against Whitechapel. Even Mr Browning was on the side of Wimpole Street and against Flush.

But Miss Barrett was stronger than all of them and one morning ordered her maid Wilson to fetch a cab. No wonder she was determined; the wicked dog-snatcher had threatened to send her Flush's ears, and then his paws, and then his head, in a neat parcel. Miss Barrett told the cabman to drive to Manning Street, Shoreditch. 'Soon they were in a world that Miss Barrett had never seen, had never guessed at. They were in a world where cows are herded under bedroom floors, where whole families sleep in rooms with broken windows.' They waited outside a public-house, while a messenger went to look for Taylor, but returned only with more promises. Miss Barrett went back to Wimpole Street, having seen what lay on the other side—those faces, those houses. 'They were to come before her again years later when she sat writing on a sunny balcony in Italy. They were to inspire the most vivid passages in *Aurora Leigh*.' Not for Flush's sake, but for Mrs Browning's, did Virginia Woolf write that Whitechapel scene three times. At last, Flush, emaciated and still terrified, is safely back with his mistress in Wimpole Street; and thanks to him we have had a glimpse of the London slums of the 1840's. Orlando did not see them, and *The Years* begins in 1880.

Years after their elopement, the Brownings came back from Italy for a visit, and lodged in Welbeck Street, not far from Wimpole Street, and Flush refreshed his impresssions of London. 'All Welbeck Street . . . was wrapped in a splendour of red light—a light not clear and fierce like the Italian light, but tawny and troubled with the dust of a million wheels, with the trampling of a million hooves. The London season was at its height. A pall of sound, a cloud of interwoven humming, fell over the city in one confluent growl. By came a majestic deer-hound led on a chain by a page. A policeman, swinging past with rhythmical stride, cast his bull's eye from side to side. Odours of stew, odours of beef, odours of bastings, odours of beef and cabbage rose from a thousand basements.' No more of the freedom of the streets of Florence for Flush, but confinement and walking on a leash. The pointers and setters of Wimpole Street welcomed Flush and overlooked the condition of his coat, somewhat damaged by Italian fleas. But Flush felt that there was a certain morbidity now among the London dogs. 'It was common knowledge that Mrs Carlyle's dog Nero had leapt from a top storey window with the intention of committing suicide. He had found the strain of life in Cheyne Row intolerable.' Flush could well believe it. It is pleasant to remember that he returned to Florence to pass his old age.

VIII

The Years:
The London Novel?

The excitement over her idea of an Essay-Novel kept Virginia Woolf 'infinitely delighting in facts for a change, and in possession of quantities beyond counting: though I feel now and then the tug to vision, but resist it'. Several of the critics of *The Years* deplore this resistance to vision. Mr E. M. Forster calls it a desertion of poetry for concern with society and its problems, and he thinks her outlook on society ,however warm and shrewd, is best understood by looking at a 'very peculiar side of her: her Feminism'. Male critics generally do not like that, and yet it isn't so very peculiar, at least as Orlando understood it. Mr David Daiches refers to her aloofness from the problems of the day. So, apparently, she is at the same time too aloof and too concerned. While she was working on *The Years*, Europe was drifting ever closer to catastrophe. Ralph Bates remembers how in June, 1936, at a group discussion of the role of the artist in the crisis—a group including Malraux, Ralph Fox, and Ernst Toller—Mrs Woolf listened 'with profound anxiety to every word and recounted experience out of that Europe from which England still seemed removed . . . More than most writers she knew the spiritual predicament of England.' And she was more vulnerable because she was 'unprotected by the carapace of dogmatism which many of us possessed'.* However one may

* Ralph Bates, in the New York Herald-Tribune *Books*, Sept. 30, 1945.

characterize the attitude towards the problems of society in *The Years*, it cannot be called 'aloof'; test it by the section '1917'.

As the work progressed, it dawned on her that the discovery of this book was 'the combination of the external and the internal'. Such a torrent of fact was released as she didn't know she had in her; 'I must have been observing and collecting these 20 years'. One of her problems was to 'clear the truth of the unessential', to give both the facts and the vision; 'I mean, *The Waves* going on simultaneously with *Night and Day*. Is this possible?' Perhaps it was not possible to 'give the whole of society—nothing less'. Perhaps she accomplished something a little different from her professed purpose, and gave us that book about London which in 1924 she thought of writing 'one of these days'. If one reads *The Years* as continuing the earlier experiments of using London impressions in integrating the inner and outer aspects of experience, an organized and vivid design emerges of a London changing, surviving through the years, always enchanting, playing its part in the lives of the passing generations.

It is not always June in London. In *The Years* we have all seasons and weathers: autumn with wind in 1891, March with wind in 1908, November in 1918, midwinter with snow in 1913, a very cold winter's night for the air-raid-cellar scene in 1917; but nothing as spectacular as the Great Frost of *Orlando*. There is sunset at the beginning and dawn at the end, and other sunsets and dawns in between, cold clear nights and hot afternoons. People take long walks, alone or in company, ride in omnibuses from one end of the town to the other, go places in hansoms and four-wheelers and taxis. Familiar to us from the earlier books are the Strand, Hyde Park Corner, the Serpentine, the Round Pond, Oxford Street, Piccadilly, Bloomsbury, the City, the river and the bridges and St Paul's; but they are all seen freshly, usually through the eyes of one or another of the characters. And there are some parts of the city we have not visited before.

The houses where people live are realized in far greater detail than in the preceding novels. They are fully furnished shells for the life that goes on within them, with windows to look out from. The Pargiter family grew up in a house in Abercorn Terrace. (It must have been in the St John's Wood district, if the Index in the London guide of today is any clue, with its Abercorn Place and Abercorn Mews and Abercorn Close). The Pargiters lived in it from 1880 on, until, the family grown and married and scattered, it is finally sold. Another branch of the family lived in Browne Street, Westminster, in a gayer, less tidy, more interesting house, also destined to be sold. A cousin, Lady Lasswade, has a town house in Grosvenor Square. Very different are the flats and lodgings—fairly comfortable ones like Martin's in Ebury Street, and very sordid ones like Sally's in Milton Street. The final reunion of the surviving Pargiters takes place in lodgings in an old house in a square near Southampton Row.

We begin our London exploring in the West End, on an uncertain spring day at the beginning of the season in 1880. Ladies in bright dresses with bustles are shopping. Gentlemen in frock coats, carrying canes, with carnations in their button-holes, are strolling near Hyde Park Corner and in Park Lane, lifting hats to a passing Princess; and there is an incessant stream of landaus and victorias and hansom cabs. In the Park sparrows twitter, thrushes sing, and there are pigeons on the grass. In the basements of the houses in the long residential avenues servant girls in cap and apron prepared tea; 'deviously ascending from the basement the silver tea-pot was placed on the table, and virgins and spinsters with hands that had staunched the sores of Bermondsey and Hoxton carefully measured out one, two, three spoonfuls of tea'. After sundown a million little gaslights left broad stretches

85

of darkness on the pavements, and 'the mixed light of the lamps and the setting sun were reflected equally in the placid waters of the Round Pond and the Serpentine. Diners-out, trotting over the Bridge in hansom cabs, looked for a moment at the charming vista.' We shall soon enter one of the houses; Eleanor Pargiter, 'virgin and spinster', returning from a charitable visit to the East End, will come home for tea; other members of the family will drive over the Serpentine bridge on the way to evening parties.

Colonel Abel Pargiter, a retired officer, after lunch at his Club, looks down from the window into Piccadilly, on the tops of omnibuses, cabs, victorias, vans and landaus, feeling gloomy and out of sorts. His wife is dying and taking a long time about it, there are his children to bring up, everybody at the Club has some engagement. Then he remembers Mira, the lady in the little street of dingy houses under the shadow of the Abbey, who is strictly his own affair, and he sets off across the Green Park to visit her. Children scream on the pavement outside of the smelly lodging-house, a barrel organ is playing down the street, Mira's room is untidy, and it is all sordid, mean and furtive. The Colonel is uneasy, but he stays, for Mira has beautiful golden hair, even if she is nearly forty, and is kind. There is a sudden squall of rain and the children disappear. 'The elderly street singer, who had been swaying along the kerb, with a fisherman's cap stuck jauntily on the back of his head, lustily chanting 'Count your blessings, count your blessings,' turned up his coat collar and took refuge under the portico of a public-house where he finished his injunction: "Count your blessings. Every one." '

The Colonel goes home to tea, where the daughters of the house in the drawing-room are trying to get the water to boil in the brass kettle over a feeble flame. The family gather, down to the youngest, Rose; the Colonel comes in (and young Martin hastily wriggles out of his father's arm-chair); his

favourite daughter Delia asks an unfortunate question—
'Have you had any adventure, Papa?'—and finally to everyone's relief the Colonel goes out. Delia looks out of the front
window at the houses opposite, all with the same little front
gardens, the same front steps, the same pillars, the same bow
windows. 'But now dusk was falling and they looked spectral
and insubstantial in the dim light. Lamps were being lit; a
light glowed in the drawing-room opposite; then the curtains
were drawn, and the room was blotted out . . . A woman
of the lower classes was wheeling a perambulator; an old man
tottered along with his hands behind his back. Then the street
was empty; there was a pause. Here came a hansom
jingling down the road . . . Was it going to stop at their
door or not? . . . But then, to her regret, the cabman jerked
his reins, the horse stumbled on; the cab stopped two doors
lower down. "Someone's calling on the Stapletons," she
called back.'

Milly joins her sister at the window to watch a young man in
a top hat get out of the cab and run up the steps of the house,
and they stand looking at the yellow and purple crocuses in
the garden and at the sunset above the roofs, 'one of those red
and fitful London sunsets that make window after window
burn gold. There was a wildness in the spring evening; even
here, in Abercorn Terrace the light was changing from gold
to black, from black to gold.' Delia, suddenly filled with
impatience, cries out 'Oh my God!' Then the maid draws
the thick claret-coloured curtains, cutting off the world
outside.

Seven-year-old Rose, who has an errand to do at a little
shop nearby, slips out by herself and runs down the street,
imagining herself riding to the rescue of a beleaguered
garrison—she is Pargiter of Pargiter's Horse. This street
that bores her sisters happens to be dangerous for a little
girl in the gathering dusk, as the street lamps are being

lighted. The pavement stretched out before her broad and dark, with a wavering network of shadows from the trees. She had to cross a street to reach Lanly's shop. But before she could cross the imagined desert and ford the river, a man emerged from under the gas lamp and tried to stop her. Thoroughly frightened and no longer living her imagined story, she dashed past him. Her errand done, she faced the long stretch of empty street to return. 'The trees were trembling their shadows over the pavement. The lamps stood at great distances apart, and there were pools of darkness between. She began to trot.' The pervert was there, the light from the lamp flickering over 'a white, peeled, pock-marked' face. Again she was too quick for him and reached her door in safety. The nightmarish experience is buried but not forgotten.

Long after the Pargiters have left Abercorn Terrace, Eleanor, an old lady, driving with her niece to the family reunion, points out the house. 'She waved her hand towards a long lamp-starred street on the left. Peggy, looking out, could just see the imposing unbroken avenue with its succession of pale pillars and steps. The repeated columns, the orderly architecture, had even a pale pompous beauty as one stucco column repeated another stucco column all down the street. "Abercorn Terrace," said Eleanor.'

It was back in 1913, on a snowy January day, that Eleanor had taken a last look at the dismantled house with the housekeeper Crosby, who had served the family there for forty years. The snow gave everything a hard white glare through the uncurtained windows, showing up every crack and stain, every mark where pictures had hung and furniture stood. The young man from the House Agents made unflattering references to the lack of modern conveniences. Crosby followed Eleanor around like an old dog, exchanging memories with her, on the point of tears, for it was the end of everything

for her. 'She had known every cupboard, flagstone, chair and table in that large rambling house, not from five or six feet of distance as they had known it; but from her knees, as she scrubbed and polished; she had known every groove, stain, fork, knife, napkin and cupboard. They and their doings had made her entire world. And now she was going off, alone, to a single room at Richmond.' Eleanor, glad to be quit of it all, suddenly realized how dark and low the basement was, which had been Crosby's home for forty years. At last Crosby, the old dog in her arms and the snow falling on her black bonnet, climbed into the four-wheeler. But she does not pass entirely out of the book, coming in from Richmond every week to take care of the laundry of her favourite Martin.

On one of the mornings when Crosby comes to Ebury Street, to Martin's lodgings, he is standing at the window of his dark room, looking out at the mean outlines of the houses showing through the sleet, and indulging in some gloomy reflections on family life. He had recently found among his father's papers some letters from Mira; why, he wonders, had his father lied about keeping a mistress? and then he remembers some deceptions of his own. 'Family life; Abercorn Terrace. No wonder the house would not let. It had one bathroom, and a basement; and there all those different people had lived, telling lies.' But a year or so later in a brilliant spring, Martin, in the best of spirits, looks out of the same window and admires a lady in a charming hat, pausing before a curiosity shop opposite, where a blue pot is displayed on a Chinese stand against a green brocade background. Both the lady and the pot are charming. He decides to walk part of the way to the City to see his stockbroker. (Later we shall join him).

The eldest Pargiter son, Sir Digby, lives in the house on Browne Street, Westminster, with his half-French wife, Eugenie, and their two daughters, Maggie (Magdalena) and

Virginia Woolf's London

Sally (Sara). Eugenie's taste brings an exotic note into the Victorian drawing-room; some pieces of furniture, like an upholstered chair with gilt claws, survive the wreckage of time and diminished fortunes, and turn up incongruously in the dingy lodgings of the daughters. Sir Digby and his wife have an active social life. One fine evening in 1907, they are going out to dinner; Maggie is with them, but the young Sally is left at home; their cab crosses the bridge over the Serpentine, red in the setting sun. 'The trees grouped together, sculptured, losing their detail; and the ghostly architecture of the little bridge, white at the end, composed the scene. The lights —the sunlight and the artificial light—were strangely mixed.' The cab leaves the Park and joins the long line of cabs taking people to plays and dinner parties.

Sally, alone in her top back room on this summer night, is reading and reflecting and from time to time looking out on moon-lighted back gardens, into which a party is overflowing. The dance music drifting in through the open window keeps her from concentrating on her reading. She leans her elbow on the sill and watches the party. The music and the clapping stop, and people come down the iron staircase into the garden, which is marked out with blue and yellow lamps dotted along the wall. 'The dotted square of green was full of the flowing pale figures of women in evening dress; of the upright black-and-white figures of men in evening dress . . . They were talking and laughing; but they were too far off for her to hear what they were saying.' The garden of her own house was empty and silent; 'a cat slid stealthily along the top of the wall; stopped; and then went on again as if drawn on some secret errand'. (This is Westminster, not Mayfair, but the scene suggested in *Street Haunting* has come to life).

Sally has a mind given to extravagant fantasy, now allowed full play as she reads a translation of *Antigone* by her cousin Edward Pargiter, an Oxford don. The burial of Antigone on a

moonlight night mingles with the garden scene outside. She falls asleep, but the party in the garden goes on, without relation to Sally. ' "It's a lovely night," said the girl who was going up the iron steps with her partner. She rested her hand on the iron balustrade. It felt very cold. She looked up: a slice of yellow light lay around the moon.' Later, Sally's mother and sister, back from their evening party, come in to say good-night, and it is Maggie who looks out into the garden and watches the couples filling the garden with pale pinks and whites, moving in and out. The differently tinted colours 'seemed to ripple one over the other until they entered the angle where the light from the house fell, when they suddenly turned to ladies and gentlemen in full evening dress'. The bedroom scene is closed by the sound of the Abbey clock striking the hour—'softly, tumultuously, as if it were a flurry of soft sighs hurrying one on top of another, yet concealing something hard.'

Rather inexplicably—Mrs Woolf does not fill in this gap in the Pargiter history—Sir Digby and Eugenie are dead, and the year after the garden scene, the house in Browne Street is sold. Cousin Martin, back from Africa and India, stops to look at it: 'He stood for a moment gazing at the black windows now grimed with dust. It was a house of character; built sometime in the eighteenth century. Eugenie had been proud of it. And I used to like going there, he thought. But now an old newspaper was on the door-step; wisps of straw had caught in the railings; and he could see, for there were no blinds, into an empty room. A woman was peering up at him from behind the bars of a cage in the basement.'

(How often do street haunters wonder about the life that used to go on in empty houses?).

Sally and Maggie, who are poor after the breaking-up of their branch of the Pargiter family, and Eleanor, their older cousin, who does charitable work among 'the poor', make

us familiar with certain London slums. Back in the Eighties
Eleanor visits Rigby Cottages in Peter Street, a housing
improvement effort of some organization in which she is
active. The Cottages look a little different from the uniform
yellow-grey boxes with slate roofs on either side of them.
The street is smoky and dreary and nothing whatever is going
on, except for a few children playing and two cats turning
over something in the gutter with their paws. A woman is
leaning out of a window with an indolent dissatisfied stare,
'as if she were raking every cranny for something to feed on'.
She watches Eleanor come around the corner and meet a
little man, a contractor, who is to inspect one of the Cottages.
We go in with Eleanor, talk with the tenants, smell the drains,
see the leaks in the ceiling and the holes in the plaster, and
conclude with her that the poor little contractor is not much
good at his job. Knowing that she has been swindled, losing
her temper, adopting the tone of 'the Colonel's daughter'—a
tone she detests, she gets through the thankless task and catches
her bus back to Abercorn Terrace. The bus trundles along the
Bayswater Road; shops give place to houses, big and little,
private houses and public houses, and now and then a church.
'Underneath were pipes, wires, drains . . . Her lips began
moving. She was talking to herself. There's always a public
house, a library, a church, she was muttering.' A man in the
bus sizes her up as a well-known type—with a bag—philan-
thropic, well-nourished—like all the women of her class,
cold, yet not unattractive. Walking up her own street, she
notices how respectable the houses look, and seems to see in
every front room 'a parlour-maid's arm sweep over the table,
laying it for luncheon'.

This is only the beginning of Eleanor's day. After lunching
with her father, she takes a hansom cab to the Law Courts,
where her brother is to argue a case that afternoon. As the
horse keeps up a steady jog-trot down the Bayswater Road,

she reads a letter from Martin in India, recounting an exciting adventure in the jungle, and the passing scene becomes mixed-up in her fancy with her brother's story, so that when the cab stops at the Law Courts, Eleanor for moment sees stunted little trees. In the court-room she listens to the arguments as long as she can stand it, and then, slipping out, experiences a shock of relief in the uproar and confusion of the Strand, the turmoil of variegated life that comes racing towards her. Everything gives her pleasure; 'the shops full of bright chains and leather cases,' the white-faced churches, the jagged roofs laced across and across with wires. 'Above was the dazzle of a watery but gleaming sky.' How, she wonders, could her brother stand the dark Court all day? Halted by the crowd at the entrance to Charing Cross station, she reads on a placard carried by a newsboy—Parnell Dead, and remembers how passionately her sister Delia cared for Parnell's Cause. Crossing over into Trafalgar Square, she stops by the basin of water rippled black by the wind, and decides to go and see Delia. A cab drives her through some 'mean and vicious streets . . . here was the vice, the obscenity, the reality of London . . .lurid in the mixed evening light'. Stopping the cab opposite a 'little row of posts in an alley', she enters an old faded square, 'dingy and decrepit and full of mist', where the houses were let out to societies and offices, but where the house she is looking for has an old Queen Anne doorway, 'with heavy-carved eyebrows', and where the wooden stairs she climbs have carved banisters. There is no answer when she knocks at Delia's door, outside of which is an empty milk-jug. 'The traffic hummed far off . . . pigeons crooned in the tree-tops.' She could just hear the newsboys crying death-death.

This 'old square off Holborn', where Delia lives, reappears several times in *The Years*; once as the scene of a suffrage society meeting in 1910 (with Eleanor present), and again at the end of the novel when the Pargiters gather for the reunion. It is probably Red Lion Square, now (1958) changed, but not quite beyond recognition, though new office buildings have replaced most of the old houses, and at one end is a big parking lot for Seeing London Tours. On one of the still dignified houses on the south side is a plaque commemorating the residence there at different times in the 1850's of William Morris, Dante Gabriel Rossetti and Edward Burne-Jones. An entry in Mrs Woolf's *Diary* for May 31, 1928, reads: 'I walked Pinker to Gray's Inn Gardens this morning and saw —Red Lion Square; Morris's house; thought of them on winter's evenings in the 50's; thought we were just as interesting.'

Leaving Eleanor at the suffrage meeting in 1910, we find Rose, the little girl who had been frightened long ago by the man near the lamp-post, on her way to lunch with her cousins Sally and Maggie across the river. She is now forty or so. She walks over the bridge—Waterloo—pausing to look at the river from one of the little scooped-out alcoves. 'It was running fast, a muddy gold this morning, with smooth breadths and ripples, for the tide was high. And there was the usual tug and the usual barges with black tarpaulins and corn showing. The water swirled round the arches. As she stood there looking down at the water, some buried feeling began to arrange the stream into a pattern. The pattern was painful. She remembered how she had stood there on the night of a certain engagement, crying; her tears had fallen, her happiness, it seemed to her, had fallen. Then she had turned—here she turned—and had seen the churches, the masts and roofs of the city. There's *that*, she had said to herself. Indeed it was a splendid view.' Returning to the present and looking at the Houses of Parliament, Rose (who not long after this goes to jail for militant suffrage activity) exclaims, 'Damned humbugs!' to the surprise of a passing clerk.

Hyams Place, where her cousins live, is 'a little crescent of old houses with the name carved in the middle.' Mrs Woolf has extended her London to include one of those 'long streets south of the river', about whose inhabitants she speculated briefly in *A Room of One's Own.* It is shabby and noisy; a woman shouting to a neighbour, a child crying, a man wheeling a barrow and bawling his wares—bedsteads, grates, pokers and odd pieces of twisted iron—though 'whether he was selling old iron or buying old iron it was impossible to say; the rhythm persisted; but the words were almost rubbed out'. The sounds penetrate the upper room where Sally is sitting at the piano when Rose enters. A rather poverty-stricken room, Rose thinks, but she recognizes the gilt and crimson chair from the house in Westminster. The three cousins, who have seen very little of one another in recent years, carry on a rather constrained and perfunctory conversation. Rose looks out of the window: 'Opposite there was a row of slate roofs, like half-opened umbrellas; and rising above them, a great building which, save for thin black strokes across it, seemed to be made entirely of glass. It was a factory. The man bawled in the street underneath.' As they talk, the recovery of bits of the past unites this scene with earlier parts of the novel. The screaming of children in the street and the cries of the iron-to-sell-or-buy man punctuate the conversation, which has a special quality because Sally is erratic and imaginative, with a gift for mimicry. After lunch she goes off with Rose to the suffrage meeting in Red Lion Square.

Martin Pargiter, the red-headed schoolboy of 1880, after an army career in India and Africa, returns about 1907 as Captain Pargiter, to put his personal life in order—business affairs with his stockbroker and love affairs with unnamed ladies. He has lodgings in Ebury Street, where we have already met him. Martin was something of a hater when he was young, but he gradually grows mellow, and when we see the last of him 'at the present time', he is cherubic, pink and plump;

and his niece Peggy, talking with him at the family reunion, likes his 'eternal pursuit of one love after another love—his gallant clutch upon the flying tail, the slippery tail of youth—even he, even now'. He is really not a particularly interesting man, and little given to speculation or introspection; but his years away from London make him freshly and curiously observant. During a long day in the spring of 1914, his response to sights and sounds and people creates one of the most rounded and complete impressions of London in all Virginia Woolf's novels.

The day is brilliant, at the beginning of the season; 'from all the spires of all the London churches—the fashionable saints of Mayfair, the dowdy saints of Kensington, the hoary saints of the City—the hour was proclaimed. The air over London seemed a rough sea of sound through which circles travelled.' Martin, his stick swinging from side to side like the tail of a dog, decides to walk part of the way from Ebury Street to the City. He is humming a tune, an organ grinder is playing a merry jig, the shop windows he passes on his way up Sloane Street are full of summer dresses, and everybody seems light-hearted and irresponsible. At Hyde Park Corner vans, motor-cars and omnibuses are streaming down the hill, and cars with gay ladies in pale dresses are already passing in at the gates. Someone has chalked up the words 'God is Love' on the gate of Apsley House; it needs pluck, he thinks, to write that on Wellington's mansion. He takes a bus to St Paul's, where the traffic swirls round the steps, and the statue of Queen Anne seems to preside over the chaos, supplying it with a centre, like the hub of a wheel. 'It seemed as if the white lady ruled the traffic with her sceptre; directed the activities of the little men in bowler hats and round coats; of the women carrying attaché cases; of the vans, the lorries and the motor omnibuses ... The doors of the Cathedral kept opening and shutting. Now and then a blast of faint organ music was blown out into the air. The pigeons waddled; the sparrows fluttered.' And of course an old man with a paper bag full of crumbs starts feeding them and a crowd gathers to watch. When the great clock strikes One, the pigeons and sparrows flutter up into the air, and some pigeons make a little flight around Queen Anne's head.

Martin, standing with his back against a shop-window, looks up at the great dome. 'All the weights in his body seemed to shift. He had a curious sense of something moving in his body in harmony with the building; it righted itself; it came to a full stop. It was exciting—this change of proportion. He wished he had been an architect.' His effort to get the whole of the Cathedral clear is prevented by the crowds bumping into him—the City men hurrying to lunch. Catching sight of his odd cousin Sally standing against one of the pillars and being a little tired now of his own company, he taps her on the shoulder, and they look down for a moment on the crowded street—a faint ecclesiastical murmur coming from the dark space of the Cathedral behind them, as the doors open and shut.

He takes Sally (who looks like a somewhat dishevelled fowl) to a City chop-house for lunch, along a narrow alley blocked by carts into which packages were being shot from warehouses, and through swing doors into the place where he often lunched and where the joint is succulent and the wine good—so good that Sally, always over susceptible to wine and extravagant enough in her speech without stimulation, says things that embarrass Martin. When he asks what she makes of the prayer-book she has with her, she opens it and reads, 'The Father incomprehensible, the Son incomprehensible', till he hushes her. And what was *he* doing at St Paul's, she asks, and he picks up the wish that he had been an architect, 'but they sent me into the Army, which I loathed.' 'Hush.' she teases him, 'somebody's listening.'

F

Virginia Woolf's London

Sally is to meet her sister Maggie, now married to a Frenchman and with a new baby, at the Round Pond at four, and Martin decides to go with her, though he ought to visit his sister Rose in jail, where like other militant suffragettes she is being forcibly fed. The waiter tries an old trick to cheat Martin out of a couple of shillings, and Martin angrily refuses a tip, but is so uneasy about it that the pleasant sense of correspondence between his body and the stone is no longer there as he looks up at St Paul's in passing. Stepping on and off the pavement, passing people in the crowd on Fleet Street, he thinks that after all the poor devil had to make a living. The cousins laugh at 'the splayed-out figure at Temple Bar . . . something between a serpent and a fowl'; they notice the cold stone mass of the gloomy Law Courts; the sting over his handling of the waiter is dying down, but is revived when Martin sees an old beggar woman selling violets, her hat pulled down over her face which he catches sight of as he drops a sixpence in her tray—to make amends to the waiter. A scarred face, without a nose. (Another echo here of *Street Haunting*). He hurries Sally across the street, to spare her the sight of the woman's face, and buys a paper at Charing Cross, where men and women were sucked in as if they were water around the piers of a bridge. The right bus comes along, they climb to the top and are carried smoothly down the incline of Piccadilly, past the Club windows where his father used to sit. When he tries to get Sally to talk, she is absorbed in the sight of the sun blazing on the windows of St George's Hospital at Hyde Park Corner. Sally is usually absorbed in something, like tying her shoe-lace, when Martin seeks to communicate with her.

Since the morning the scene in the Park has become more festive; green chairs are drawn up at the edge of the Row and riders are cantering up and down. They start walking at random in the Park; several people whom they pass are

talking to themselves; one lady, who sees that they have
noticed her muttering, whistles to a dog as if it were hers—
only it isn't, and bounds off in another direction. 'People,'
says Sally, 'don't like being looked at when they're talking
to themselves.' She is still under the influence of the wine, of
the wandering airs, of the people passing. The soft air is 'laden
with murmurs; with the stir of branches; the rush of wheels;
dogs barking; and now and again the intermittent song of a
thrush'. Discovering presently that they have gone in the
wrong direction and have come to the 'bald rubbed space'
where the Hyde Park orators are up on their platforms, they
stop to listen. One chap, banging on the rail of his platform, is
shouting 'Fellow citizens!' to a crowd of loafers, errand boys
and nursemaids. 'Joostice and liberty,' Martin repeats. 'But
he's a jolly good speaker.' An old lady is saying something
about sparrows in a thin frail pipe of a voice, imitated by a
chorus of little boys.

They stroll on now in the right direction across the smooth
green slope of the Park. 'Great white dogs were gambolling;
through the trees shone the waters of the Serpentine, set here
and there with little boats. The urbanity of the Park, the
gleam of the water, the sweep and curve and composition of
the scene, as if somebody had designed it, affected Martin
agreeably. "Joostice and liberty," he said half to himself, as
they came to the water's edge and stood a moment, watching
the gulls cut the air into sharp white patterns with their wings.'
He would like to talk to Sara about the man and the old lady—
he could still see them in his mind—but Sara is talking to
herself. So they come to the gate into Kensington Gardens
and go on to the Round Pond through a gay scene of striped
umbrellas over tea tables and waitresses hurrying in and out
with trays, everything 'netted with floating lights from between the leaves,' pink and white chestnut blossoms moving
in the breeze, the roar of London encircling the open space

'in a ring of distant but complete sound'. 'The sun dappling the leaves gave everything a curious look of insubstantiality as if it were broken into separate points of light.'

The scene which follows, including Maggie and her baby in its pram, and Sally and Martin, is as close to Impressionist art as writing can come. It was many times rewritten. 'What I want to do,' the *Diary* records, 'is to reduce it all so that each sentence, though perfectly natural dialogue, has a great pressure of meaning behind it. And the most careful harmony and contrast of scene—the boats colliding, etc.—has also to be arranged.' It is a Conversation Piece and a Landscape with Figures. A pressure of meaning is behind the talk of the two long-separated cousins, Maggie and Martin, with its confidences exchanged and memories revived and undertsanding promoted. As for Sara, much of the time she, like the baby, is comfortably asleep, folded 'like a grasshopper with her back against a tree'.

Martin's confidences include an ordinary but painful story of his love affair with a possessive lady from whom he would like to be free; and as he tells it, the sting is drawn, though Maggie says almost nothing by way of comment. 'The baby was asleep; Sara was asleep; the presence of the two sleepers seemed to enclose them in a circle of privacy . . . The boats were sailing; the men walking; the little boys dabbled in the pond for minnows; the waters of the pond rippled bright blue.' Martin tells her also about his father's mistress and Maggie is amused. He asks her whether his father was in love with Maggie's mother, the beautiful Eugenie. The question at first doesn't reach her—she is watching the gulls; when it does she laughs out loud and asks, 'Are we brother and sister?' That wakens the baby. They look at the admirably composed scene before them: 'There was the white figure of Queen Victoria against a green bank; beyond was the red brick of the old palace; the phantom Church raised its spire, and the

Round Pond made a pool of blue. A race of yachts was going forward. The boats leant on their sides so that the sails touched the water.'

When the clocks strike Five, they wake Sara up, and Martin, who is to dine with his cousin Lady Lasswade in Grosvenor Square that evening, leaves them. Looking back he sees them still sitting by the pram under the trees. 'A very stout old lady was being tugged along the path by a small dog on a chain.'

Martin's evening at his cousin Kitty's dinner-party is as crowded with impressions as his day had been, but his mood is no longer tranquil, but tinged with detachment and cynicism. It all seems very artificial and hollow: the house itself, so correct in all its details, the guests old and young, the 'right' people, the fixed conventions, the perfect hostess. His dinner partner, a young girl of a generation from which he is rapidly receding, makes him feel middle-aged and awkward. What on earth am I going to say to her, he thinks as he gives her his arm to go down to dinner. He would like her to say of this evening —What a charming man I sat next to!—and he tries his best to break off little pieces of his vast experience to entertain her with, only to notice how she talks to the young man on her other side as if she had always known him. He wonders what her world is. Yet this world around the table is after all a good world, and very nice-looking. 'Dinner was drawing to an end. They all looked as if they had been rubbed with wash leather, like precious stones; yet the bloom seemed ingrained; it went through the stone. And the stone was clear-cut; there was no blur, no indecision.' When an awkward movement by a footman knocks over a glass of wine on a lady's dress, she does not move a muscle but goes on talking, and Martin admires that.

The ladies rise and leave the gentlemen, and we follow Lady Lasswade to the drawing-room and share the viewpoint of the hostess, watching her party. The oldest lady is her special concern; noticing that the fire is too hot for her, Lady Lass-wade opens a window, and 'just for the moment, as the curtains hung apart, she looked at the square outside. There was a spatter of leaf-shadow and lamplight on the pavement; the usual policeman was balancing himself as he patrolled; the usual little men and women, foreshortened from this height, hurried along by the railings. So she saw them hurrying, the other way, when she brushed her teeth in the morning. Then she came back and sat on a low stool beside old Aunt War-burton. The worldly old woman was honest, in her way.' A little later Aunt Warburton feels the draught from the open window, and as Lady Lasswade goes to close it, she says under her breath, ' "Damn these women!" . . . She would have liked to fleece them of their clothes, of their jewels, of their intrigues, of their gossip. The window went up with a jerk.' Ann, the girl in white satin whom Martin had failed to interest, is placed by the watchful hostess on a footstool at the hairy old dowager's knee, and the contrast stirs a moment's pity as Lady Lasswade thinks that by and by Ann will look like the other women. And yet the women of this class are brave and generous; so she comes to the same rather grudging conclusion as Martin had.

Conversation takes a new turn when the gentlemen come in. A distinguished old man lets himself slowly into a chair beside Lady Warburton, 'with the air of a ship making port', and they begin to talk as if continuing a conversation left unfinished the night before. Kitty reflects that there was something—'was it human? civilized? she could not find the word she wanted—about the old couple, talking as they had talked for the past fifty years'. Lady Kitty and Martin—through whose eyes, separately, we have taken in the party—come together briefly in an exchange of the teasing banter characteristic of their relationship, which has much of old family affection in it. He rather wants to hurt her by making fun of all this social artificiality and this conventional drawing-room. 'That's a horrid daub of you over the mantelpiece,' he says. 'I was asking myself . . . why have a picture like that . . . when they've a Gainsborough.' 'And why,' she dropped her voice, imitating his half sneering, half humorous tone, 'come and eat their food when you despise them?' They really want to talk to each other, but Kitty, seeing something wrong in the disposition of her party, leaves him.

At last 'there was a general rising and movement, like the flutter of white-winged gulls'. Most of the guests were going on to some other party. Last to leave is old Lady Warburton. Martin, dismissed by his cousin with what he feels is a perfunctory invitation to come again and see her alone, follows the old lady down the stairs, lingering a little, looking at a Canaletto on the wall—'a nice picture; but a copy, he said to himself'—and reflecting that the party had 'worked' off and on, but was it worth it? As the footman helps him with his coat, he glances through the open double doors into the street. One or two passersby peer in curiously at the footman, the bright hall, and the old lady, 'who paused for a moment on the black-and-white squares. She was robing herself. Now she was accepting her cloak with a violet slash in it; now her furs. A bag dangled from her wrist. She was hung about with chains; her fingers were knobbed with rings. Her sharp stone-coloured face, riddled with lines and wrinkled into creases, looked out from its soft nest of furs and laces. The eyes were still bright. The nineteenth century going to bed, Martin said to himself as he watched her hobble down the steps on the arm of her footman.'

So ends Martin's day, which in this London dinner-party has given us a small Proustian panel—with the interplay of personalities, the shifting moods, the feeling for age, middle-age and youth, the sharply etched background, the broken dialogue, the carefully controlled points of view, the implied social criticism, and the touches of doubt and compassion and admiration that qualify the satire. An age is passing. London will never be quite like that again. And it seems appropriate at this point to leave London with Lady Lasswade at midnight, with a deep sigh of relief. She is tired. Even London can be exhausting.

Having seen the last of her guests depart and dismissed her maid, Lady Lasswade is driven by her chauffeur to the station, to catch the midnight train to the North, to her estate in Yorkshire. On this still clear night every tree in Grosvenor Square was visible: 'Some were black, others were sprinkled with strange patches of green artificial light. Above the arc lamps rose shafts of darkness. Although it was close on midnight, it scarcely seemed to be night; but rather some ethereal disembodied day, for there were so many lamps in the streets; cars passing; men in white mufflers with their light overcoats open walking along the clean dry pavements, and many houses were still lit up, for everyone was giving parties. The town changed as they drew smoothly through Mayfair. The public houses were closing; here was a group clustered round a lamp-post at the corner. A drunken man was bawling out some loud song; a tipsy girl with a feather bobbing in her eyes was swaying as she clung to the lamp-post.' Kitty's mind, exhausted by the efforts of the evening, adds nothing to this picture of London by night. But when she walks along the station platform, exhilaration begins to mount. 'Men's cries and the clangour of shunting carriages echoed in the immense vacancy. The train was waiting; travellers were making ready to start . . . She looked down the length of the train and saw the engine sucking water from a hose. It seemed all body, all muscle; even the neck had been consumed into the smooth barrel of the body. This was "the" train; the others were toys in comparison. She sniffed up the sulphurous air . . . as if it already had a tang of the North.'

The Years: The London Novel

As a frequent traveller on the train, Kitty is known to the guard, who unlocks the door of her carriage; everything is ready in the small lighted compartment. 'Then the train gave a gentle tug. She could hardly believe that so great a monster could start so gently on so long a journey. Then she saw the tea-urn sliding past . . . All the tension went out of her body. She was alone; and the train was moving. The last lamp on the platform slid away. The last figure on the platform vanished. "What fun", she said to herself, as if she were a little girl who had run away from her nurse and escaped.' Jerking up the blind she watches the lights slide past—lights in factories and warehouses and obscure back streets, lights in public gardens. 'They were leaving London behind them; leaving that blaze of light which seemed, as the train rushed into the darkness, to contract itself into one fiery circle. The train rushed with a roar through a tunnel.' So Kitty passes from one world to another. She draws down the blind, catching a glimpse of a group of cows, a hedge of hawthorn. She drifts into reverie and finally into sleep.

The world she steps out into the next morning is totally different from her London world. After breakfast and a stroll on the terrace she walks through the woods to a high place, from which she sees the country spread wide all around her. 'Her body seemed to shrink; her eyes to widen. She threw herself on the ground, and looked over the billowing land that went rising and falling, away and away, until somewhere far off it reached the sea . . . Dark wedges of shadow, bright breadths of light lay side by side. Then, as she watched, light moved and dark moved; light and shadow went travelling over the hills and over the valleys. A deep murmur sang in her ears—the land itself, a chorus, alone. She lay there listening. She was happy, completely. Time had ceased.'

This is another music than that of the London streets.

IX

The Years:

The Present Day

Before the curtain rises on the present day, the last long section of *The Years*, there is the briefest of glimpses of the London of the war years, on a winter night in 1917. It is an interlude; a little gathering at the house in an obscure street under the Abbey where Maggie, her French husband, and their children live. With them for dinner are Eleanor, Sally, and a Polish friend, Nicholas. There is an air raid during which they take shelter in the cellar, and the talk, with its undercurrent of fear and anxiety and its surface trivialities, reveals in sudden flashes different emotional and intellectual attitudes towards the war and its problems. It is late when the bugles signal the end of the raid. Eleanor looks out through the parted curtains at the houses opposite, still curtained. 'The cold winter's night was almost black. It was like looking into the hollow of a dark blue stone. Here and there a star pierced the blue. She had a sense of immensity and peace—as if something had been consumed.' Asked if she wants a cab, she replies, 'No, I'll walk . . . I like walking in London.'

She follows the others down the dark little street. 'A broad fan of light, like the sail of a windmill, was sweeping across the sky. It seemed to take what she was feeling and to express it broadly and simply, as if another voice were speaking in another language. Then the light stopped and examined a fleecy patch of sky, a suspected spot.' For a moment she had forgotten the raid. Victoria Street looked wider and darker than usual, with hurrying little figures emerging for a moment in the light of a lamp. She waited for an omnibus; 'a great form loomed up through the darkness; its lights were shrouded with blue paint. Inside silent people sat huddled up; they looked cadaverous and unreal in the blue light . . . The omnibus moved on. She found herself staring at an old man in the corner who was eating something out of a paper bag. He looked up and caught her staring at him. "Like to see what I've got for supper, Lady?" ' He shows her a hunk of bread with a slice of cold meat or sausage.

'This last chapter,' wrote Mrs Woolf in her *Diary*, 'must equal in length and importance and volume the first book: and must in fact give the other side, the submerged side of that.' We can expect then much less of the external in the final section. Conversations during the family reunion serve to bring the submerged to the surface. During that long evening groups of Pargiters old and young, with a few friends not of the family, form and separate and reform; couples stand apart and exchange memories of the past and comments on the present; individuals, feeling for the moment out of it, withdraw to a corner or look out of a window and enlighten us with their reveries. London is there outside. Several members of the family have come to the party from distant parts of the city, and their journeys have added a few more impressions of the London streets.

North, of the younger generation of Pargiters, drives in his sports car from the West End to have dinner with his Aunt Sally in her shabby lodgings on Milton Street, near the Prison Tower, before escorting her to the reunion. Only recently back from his African farm and unused to London traffic, he is hooted at by horns and distracted by street cries and amazed at the marvels in shop windows. All those years in

Africa he had been used to raw goods—hides and fleeces. Nearing Sally's part of town, he looks down the long vista of a street: 'Door after door, window after window, repeated the same pattern. There was a red-yellow glow over it all, for the sun was sinking through the London dust. Everything was tinged with a warm yellow haze. Barrows full of fruit and flowers were drawn up at the kerb. The sun gilded the fruit; the flowers had a blurred brilliance; there were roses, carnations and lilies too.' He thinks of buying a bunch for Sally, but the horns are hooting behind him.

Milton Street looks very sordid; many names and bells are on the door of Sally's house; through curious smells of cooking he climbs stairs with carved banisters, daubed over with cheap varnish; and her rooms are as shabby as the approach to them. But her conversation is as extravagant and fanciful as ever. While they wait for the lodging-house slavey to serve the meal, she tells him about going to a City office to present a letter of introduction. She had had a most unappetizing lodging-house breakfast and a still more unappetizing bath in a shared lodging-house bathroom, the unemployed meanwhile singing hymns under the window. 'And I said to myself—she flung her hand out, "polluted city, unbelieving city, city of dead fish and worn-out frying-pans"—thinking of a river's bank, when the tide's out, she explained . . . So I put on my hat and coat and rushed out in a rage . . . and stood on the bridge, and said, "Am I a weed, carried this way, that way, on a tide that comes twice a day without a meaning?" . . . And there were people passing; the strutting; the tiptoeing; the pasty; the ferret-eyed; the bowler-hatted, servile innumerable army of workers. And I said, "Must I join your conspiracy? Stain the hand, the unstained hand," he could see her hand gleam as she waved it in the half-light of the sitting room, "and sign on, and serve a master . . ." ' Sally's London has become the Waste Land.

The Years: The Present Day

While the slatternly maid sets out the unattractive meal, North strolls to the window and watches the effect of the setting sun on the brick house at the corner. 'One or two high windows were burnished gold . . . Against the dull background of traffic noises, of wheels turning and brakes squeaking, there rose near at hand the cry of a woman suddenly alarmed for her child; the monotonous cry of a man selling vegetables; and far away a barrel organ was playing. It stopped; it began again; I used to write to her, he thought, late at night, when I felt lonely, when I was young.'

When they leave for the party, the house has become quiet and the uproar of the day has died away. 'The vegetable-sellers, the organ-grinders, the woman practising her scales, the man playing the trombone, had all trundled away their barrows, pulled down their shutters, and closed the lids of their pianos. It was so still for a moment North thought he was back in Africa.'

North's sister Peggy calls for Aunt Eleanor at her flat in a new housing project, with modern conveniences. While waiting for the taxi to come, they look at the view high over the roofs, 'over the squares and angles of back gardens to the blue line of hills in the distance . . . The sun was setting; one cloud lay curled like a red feather in the blue . . . It was queer to see cabs turning corners, going round this street and down the other, and not to hear the sound they made. It was like a map of London; a section laid beneath them. The summer day was fading; lights were being lit, primrose lights, still separate, for the glow of the sunset was still in the sky. Eleanor pointed at the sky. "That's where I saw my first aeroplane—there between those chimneys." she said. There were high chimneys, factory chimneys, in the distance; and a great building—Westminster Cathedral, was it? — over there riding above the roofs.' Eleanor, glancing at the newspaper, sees a picture, exclaims angrily 'Damned bully!' and tears the paper across, shocking her niece, who thinks, 'It was as if she still believed with passion—she, old Eleanor—in the things that man has destroyed. A wonderful generation . . .' Later in the taxi Eleanor explains, 'It means the end of everything we cared for.' 'Freedom?' says Peggy perfunctorily. 'Yes. Freedom and justice.' Eleanor, seventy, with all her thousands of doors opening into the past, is still more hopeful of the present than Peggy, who feels older than her aunt.

They drive across London, Peggy still marvelling at her aunt's generation, believers; 'two sparks of life enclosed in two separate bodies are at this moment, she thought, driving past a picture palace. But what is this moment; and what are we?' They pass a pallid hoary-looking church and then the statue of Nurse Cavell, the lights shining on its 'cadaverous pallor'. Eleanor in her turn is shocked when Peggy remarks that it reminds her of an advertisement for sanitary towels; but Peggy is a doctor, Eleanor remembers, and one of her brothers was killed in the war. For all her surface hardness, Peggy is deeply sensitive, as we realize from time to time during the evening, when we see the party through her eyes. Both she and Eleanor are more aware than the others of the world outside. In a moment of quiet, Peggy hears the sounds of the London night—the hoot of a horn, the wail of a siren on the river—and they bring the suggestion of other worlds, indifferent to this world. She thinks of placards with Death on them at every street corner, of brutality and torture, the end of freedom, the fall of civilization. 'We here, she thought, are only sheltering under a leaf, which will be destroyed.'

The party goes on all night. Towards the end it is Eleanor who stands at the window, 'looking at the curtained houses across the square. The windows were spotted with gold. Everything looked clean swept, virginal. The pigeons were shuffling on the tree tops.' The sky was a faint blue, the roofs tinged purple against the blue, the chimneys a pure brick red. ' "And all the tubes have stopped and all the omnibuses," she said turning round . . . A breeze went through the square. In the stillness they could hear the branches rustle as they rose slightly, and fell, and shook a wave of green light through the air.' Looking out of the window again while the younger people gather their hats and cloaks, Eleanor watches a taxi gliding slowly round the square. 'It stopped in front of a house two doors down . . . A young man had got out; he paid the driver. Then a girl in a tweed travelling suit followed him. He fitted his latch-key to the door. "There," Eleanor murmured, as he opened the door and they stood for a moment on the threshold.' (So the two who drove off in the taxi in *A Room of One's Own* have come home).

'The sun had risen, and the sky above the houses wore an air of extraordinary beauty, simplicity and peace.' Eleanor thinks that there must be another life, not in dreams, 'but here and now, in this room with living people. She felt as if she were standing on the edge of a precipice with her hair blown back; she was about to grasp something that just evaded her. There must be another life, here and now, she repeated. This is too short, too broken. We know nothing, even about ourselves. We're only just beginning, she thought, to understand, here and there. She hollowed her hands in her lap . . . She held her hands hollowed; she felt that she wanted to enclose the present moment; to make it stay; to fill it fuller and fuller, with the past, the present, and the future, until it shone, whole, bright, deep with understanding.'

With the end of *The Years*, the London design may be considered complete. *Between the Acts* (1941) adds a few more street cries, a few names that are like echoes, and a London policeman directing traffic at Hyde Park Corner in the great days of Queen Victoria. The street cries are played on a gramophone during an interval in the historical pageant given on the terrace of a country house. 'Sweet lavendar . . . sweet lavendar', hums one of the ladies in the audience, and they recall the curtains blowing, the men crying—'All a blowing, all a growing'—as they came down the street with geraniums and sweet williams in pots. The tune on the record changed to 'Any old iron, any old iron to sell?' That was what the men had shouted in the fog. 'Seven Dials they came from. Men with red handkerchiefs. Garotters, did they call them? You couldn't walk—O dear me, no—home from the play. Regent Street. Piccadilly. Hyde Park Corner. The loose women . . . And everywhere loaves of bread in the gutter. The Irish you know round Covent Garden . . .'

The constable directing traffic at Hyde Park Corner in the pageant is a 'very fine figure of a man,' his truncheon extended, his waterproof pendant. 'It only wanted a shower of rain, a flight of pigeons round his head, and the pealing bells of St Paul's and the Abbey to transform him into the very spit and image of a Victorian constable; and to transport them to a foggy London afternoon, with the muffin bells ringing and the church bells pealing at the very height of Victorian prosperity.'

X

Epilogue: *A Writer's Diary*

November 3, 1936, Mrs Woolf, having given the proofs of
The Years to her husband, took what sounds like a rather
dreary walk from Tavistock Square. 'It was cold and dry and
very grey and I went out and walked through the graveyard
with Cromwell's daughter's tomb down through Gray's Inn
along Holborn and so back.* Now I was no longer Virginia,
the genius, but only a perfectly magnificent yet content—
shall I call it spirit? A body? And very tired. Very old.'

Walking in London continued to stimulate her imagination
as it had in the past; as she had noted in 1928 (May 31):
'London itself perpetually attracts, stimulates, gives me a play,
a story and a poem without any trouble, save that of moving
my legs through the streets.' In March, 1937, she made a
belated discovery in Covent Garden: 'found St Paul's, C.G.,
for the first time, heard the old char singing as she cleaned
the chairs in the ante hall.' June 22, 1937: 'If I could think
out another adventure. Oddly enough I see it now ahead of
me—in Charing Cross Road yesterday—as to do with books;
some new combination.' There were still sights that made
her 'leap with pleasure'—such as purple and grey clouds in
the evening above Regent's Park, 'with the violet and yellow
sky signs'. But other sights carried grim warnings: Spanish
refugees (June 23, 1937)—'a shuffling trudging procession,
flying—impelled by machine gun in Spanish fields to trudge

*It is Richard Cromwell's daughter, and the tomb is in St George's
Gardens north of Brunswick Square.

through Tavistock Square, along Gordon Square, then where?
—clasping their enamel kettles'.

After August 1939 she lived when in London in Mecklenburgh Square, but was often in the country at Rodmell.
On February 2, 1940, thinking of threatened London, she
wrote: 'Odd how often I think with what is love I suppose of
the City: of the walk to the Tower: that is my England: I mean,
if a bomb destroyed one of those little alleys with the brass
bound curtains and the river smell and the old woman reading,
I should feel—well, what the patriots feel.' Just back from a
trip to London (February 18): 'Bitter cold. This shortened
my walk, which I meant to be through crowded streets. Then
the dark—no lighted windows, depressed me. Standing in
Whitehall, I said to my horses "Home, John," and drove
back in the grey dawn light, the cheerless spectral light of
fading evening in houses—so much more cheerless than the
country evening—to Holborn, and so to the bright cave, which
I liked better, having shifted the chairs. How silent it is there
—and London silent: a great dumb ox, lying couchant.'

In the country and needing to think of something liberating
(March 29, 1940): 'What shall I think of? The river. Say the
Thames at London Bridge: and buying a notebook; and then
walking along the Strand and letting each face give me a
buffet; and each shop; and perhaps a Penguin.' From September, 1940, on, the London entries are a record of disaster. On
September 10, after half a day spent in London, where she
saw, thirty yards from her own house in Mecklenburgh
Square, a house demolished by a bomb, nothing remaining
but a great pile of bricks, she wrote: 'underneath all the
people who had gone down to their shelter. Scraps of cloth
hanging to the bare walls at the side still standing. A looking
glass I think swinging.' Going on to Gray's Inn, she left
the car and saw Holborn: 'A vast gap at the top of Chancery
Lane. Smoking still. Some great shop entirely destroyed: the

hotel opposite like a shell. In a wine shop there were no windows left. People standing at the tables—I think drink being served. Heaps of blue green glass in the road at Chancery Lane.' The next day, in her *Diary*, she quotes Churchill— 'our majestic City'—'which touches me, for I feel London majestic'. Disaster moved closer when the news came that all the windows in their house were broken, the ceilings down, and the china smashed. They spent the day of the 23rd in London, a lovely September day, examining the dust and the ceiling.

Then, as she noted October 20, 1940, after a trip to London, she saw an impressive sight—'the queue, mostly children with suitcases, outside Warren Street tube,' about 11.30 in the morning, and still there in a longer line with men and women and more bags and blankets, still sitting at three in the afternoon, lining up for shelter during the night's raid. Tavistock Square, where they had lived, was a heap of ruins, three houses gone, the basement all rubble; 'one glass door in the next house hanging. I could see just a piece of my studio wall standing; otherwise rubble where I wrote so many books . . . Open air where we sat so many nights, gave so many parties.' At the Mecklenburgh Square house they salvaged a few books, silver, china; and she felt an odd exhilaration at losing possessions—'save at times I want my books and chairs and carpets and beds. How I worked to buy them—one by one and the pictures . . . But it's odd— the relief at losing possessions.'

And finally there are two entries in January 1941. January 1: 'On Sunday night, as I was reading about the Great Fire, in a very accurate detailed book, London was burning. Eight of my city churches destroyed, and the Guildhall.' January 9: 'We were in London on Monday. I went to London Bridge. I looked at the river; very misty; some tufts of smoke, perhaps from burning houses. There was another fire on Saturday.

Virginia Woolf's London

Then I saw a cliff of wall, eaten out, at one corner; a great corner all smashed; a Bank; the monument erect; tried to get a bus; but such a block I dismounted; and the second bus advised me to walk. A complete jam of traffic; for streets were being blown up. So by Tube to the Temple; and there wandered in the desolate ruins of my old squares: gashed; dismantled; the old red bricks all white powder, something like a builder's yard. Grey dirt and broken windows. Sight-seers; all that completeness ravished and demolished.'

The long perspective in which this devastation would take its place, and that not the final place, was not granted to Virginia Woolf's vision. There are no further references to London in the published *Diary*. Rather grimly, March 8, 1941, she marks Henry James's sentence: 'Observe perpetually.' 'I insist on spending this time to the best advantage. I will go down with my colours flying. This I see verges on introspection; but doesn't quite fall in. Suppose I bought a ticket at the Museum; biked in daily and read history . . .'

'Jacob's mind continued onwards, alone, into the darkness.'

Bibliography

Novels, essays, reviews, by Virginia Woolf, referred to in the text, listed in chronological order.

For bibliographical details, consult *A Bibliography of Virginia Woolf*, by B. J. Kirkpatrick. Rupert Hart-Davis, London, 1957.

1905 'Street Music'. *National Review*, London.

1908 'The Stranger in London'. *Times Literary Supplement*, London.

1915 *The Voyage Out*. Duckworth & Co., London.

1916 'London Revisited'. *Times Literary Supplement*, London.

1919 *Kew Gardens*. Hogarth Press, London.

1919 *Night and Day*. Duckworth & Co., London.

1919 'The Novels of Defoe'. *Times Literary Supplement*, London. (Reprinted in *The Common Reader*, 1925).

1920 'The Letters of Henry James'. *Times Literary Supplement*, London. (Reprinted in *The Death of the Moth*, 1942).

1922 *Jacob's Room*. Hogarth Press, London.

1924 *Mr Bennett and Mrs Brown*. Hogarth Press, London. (Reprinted in *The Captain's Death Bed*, 1950).

1925 'Modern Fiction', in *The Common Reader*.

1925 *Mrs Dalloway*. Hogarth Press, London.

1927 'Street Haunting : A London Adventure'. *Yale Review*. (Reprinted in *The Death of the Moth*, 1942).

1928 *Orlando: A Biography*. Hogarth Press, London.

Virginia Woolf's London

1929   *A Room of One's Own*. Hogarth Press, London.

1931   *The Waves*. Hogarth Press, London.

1932   'Leslie Stephen; The Philosopher at Home.' *The Times*, London. (Reprinted in *The Captain's Death Bed*, 1950).

1933   *Flush: A Biography*. Hogarth Press, London.

1937   *The Years*. Hogarth Press, London.

1941   *Between the Acts*. Hogarth Press, London.

1950   'Flying over London.' (Reprinted in *The Captain's Death Bed*).

1953   *A Writer's Diary*, being extracts from the Diary of Virginia Woolf, edited by Leonard Woolf. Hogarth Press, London.

Index

Abercorn Terrace, 85, 87, 88, 92
Addison, Joseph, 59, 61, 64
Admiralty Arch, 68

Bayswater, 20, 92
Bates, Ralph, 83
Bell, Clive, 39
Between the Acts, 28, 43, 111-112
Big Ben, 10, 35, 47, 49, 50
Blackfriars, 58, 60, 63
Bloomsbury, 17, 22, 41, 67, 84
Bolt Court, 8, 61
Bond Street, 38, 48, 49
British Museum, 9, 36, 40, 45-47, 67-68, 116
Brook Street, 49
Browne Street, Westminster, 85, 89, 90, 91
Browning, Elizabeth Barrett, 79, 81
Browning, Robert, 68, 79, 81
Buckingham Palace, 51, 62

Chancery Lane, 54, 114-115
Charing Cross, 47, 63, 93, 98
Charing Cross Road, 20, 22, 29, 36, 37, 113
Chelsea, 10, 29, 32, 33, 34
Cheyne Row, 82
City of London, 19, 33, 41, 73, 84, 96, 114
Clarges Street, 11
Cockspur Street, 47
Conrad, Joseph, 28 (*Heart of Darkness*)
Constantinople, 26, 56, 59, 65
Covent Garden, 112, 113
Curzon Street, 65

Daiches, David, 83
Defoe, Daniel, 8, 9
Dickens, Charles, 7, 9 (*Bleak House*)
Duke of York Street, 19

East End, 27, 86
Ebury Street, 85, 89, 95
Eliot, T. S., 10, 108
Embankment, the, 23, 26, 29, 30, 31, 34, 37, 75
Euston, 71

Fleet Street, 18, 60, 98

Flush: A Biography, 78-82
Forster, E. M., 83
Foundling Hospital, 20
Frith Street, 11

Gerrard Street, 60
Gordon Square, 114
Gray's Inn, 94, 113, 114
Great Ormond Street, 46
Great Russell Street, 46
Green Park, 25, 48, 49, 50-51, 86
Greenwich, 29, 38, 57, 75
Grosvenor Road, 34
Grosvenor Square, 85, 101, 104

Hampstead, 58, 62
Hampton Court, 29, 38, 39, 76
Hardy, Thomas, 30
Harley Street, 48, 52
Haymarket, 49, 60, 67
Highgate, 29, 33, 58
Holborn, 22, 41, 93, 113, 114
Holtby, Winifred, 40, 70
Hungerford Bridge, 8, 9
Hyams Place, 94-95
Hyde Park, 10, 40, 41, 45, 64, 98-99
Hyde Park Corner, 25, 84, 85, 96, 98, 111, 112
Hyde Park Gate, 57

Jacob's Room, 40-47, 67
James, Henry, 11, 24-25, 116
Jermyn Street, 19
Johnson, Dr., 7, 8, 33, 43, 61

Kensington, 18, 20, 31, 96
Kensington Gardens, 19, 25, 99-100
Kensington Palace, 9, 45
Kew Gardens, 39, 40
Kew Gardens, 29, 30, 38, 65
Kingsway, 9, 28, 29, 32, 35
Knightsbridge, 18
Knole, 56, 58

Lamb's Conduit Street, 41
Law Courts, 93, 98
Leicester Square, 60
Lincoln's Inn Fields, 29, 32, 35

Index

London Bridge, 10, 59, 114, 115
Lucas, E. V., 19-20

Marble Arch, 25
Mark on the Wall, The, 39
Marylebone Road, 50
Mayfair, 22, 23, 48, 60, 62, 64, 96, 104
Mecklenburgh Square, 114, 115
Milton Street, 85, 107, 108
Modern Fiction, 7
Monument, The, 59, 116
Mr Bennett and Mrs Brown, 7
Mrs Dalloway, 17, 28, 35, 36, 48-55

Night and Day, 8, 17, 29-39, 43, 84

Orlando, 8, 11, 33, 43, 55, 56-67, 71, 84
Oxford Street, 19, 40, 41, 52, 66, 84

Park Lane, 9, 65, 85
Parliament, Houses of, 34, 94
Parliament Hill, 10, 40
Peter Street, 92
Piccadilly, 19, 25, 50, 52, 84, 86, 98
Piccadilly Circus, 27, 60, 75
Pope, Alexander, 59-60

Red Lion Square, 93-94, 95, 111
Regent Street, 49, 52, 67
Regent's Park, 29, 48, 49, 50, 52, 80, 113
Richmond, 25, 89
Room of One's Own, A, 55, 67-70, 95, 111
Round Pond, 25, 84, 86, 99-101
Russell Square, 19, 21, 29, 31, 35, 36, 38, 52
St. Giles-in-the-Fields, 20
St James's Park, 62
St Martin-in-the-Fields, 20
St Paul's, 9, 10, 40, 41, 43, 54, 59, 62, 75-76, 84, 96-97
Serpentine, The, 25, 45, 64, 84, 86, 90, 99
Shaftsbury Avenue, 75
Shoreditch, 81
Sloane Street, 96

Soho, 22, 40, 44, 45
Southampton Row, 17, 21, 29, 35, 78, 85
Stanhope Gate, 65
Stephen, Sir Leslie, 25, 57
Strand, The, 9, 23, 29, 35, 36, 43, 47, 54, 60, 63, 75, 84, 93, 114
Street Haunting, 21-23, 90, 98

Tavistock Square, 17, 21, 113, 114, 115
Temple, The, 29, 34, 54, 116
Temple Bar, 32, 98
Thames, 10, 26, 27, 30, 43, 56, 57, 59, 94, 114
Times Literary Supplement, 8, 24, 33
To the Lighthouse, 35, 48
Tottenham Court Road, 80
Tower, The, 62
Tower Bridge, 27
Trafalgar Square, 9, 75, 93

Underground Railways, 10, 35, 40, 74

Victoria, Queen, 25, 51, 62
Victoria Street, 49, 53, 107
Voyage Out, The, 26, 59

Waterloo Bridge, 10, 23, 26, 29, 31, 40, 42, 94
Waves, The, 10, 22, 71-77, 78, 84
Welbeck Street, 81-82
West End, 27, 80, 107
Westminster, 26, 35, 48
Westminster Abbey, 52, 59, 62, 86, 91, 106
Westminster Bridge, 9, 10, 67
Westminster Cathedral, 109
Whitechapel, 80, 81
Whitehall, 40, 47, 49, 51, 114
Wimpole Street, 79, 81, 82
Wordsworth, William, 9
Writer's Diary, A, 7, 8, 17, 78, 94, 100, 107, 113-116

Years, The, 10, 18, 22, 78, 81, 83-112, 113

83
85